CLEARING
THE HIGH
HURDLES

OVERCOMING OBSTACLES TO OBEYING GOD'S CALL

BIBLE STUDY GUIDE

From the Bible-teaching ministry of

Charles R. Swindoll

INSIGHT FOR LIVING

Chuck graduated in 1963 from Dallas Theological Seminary, where he now serves as the school's fourth president, helping to prepare a new generation of men and women for the ministry. Chuck has served in pastorates in three states: Massachusetts, Texas, and California, including almost twenty-three years at the First Evangelical Free Church in Fullerton, California. His sermon messages have been aired over radio since 1979 as the *Insight for Living* broadcast. A best-selling author, Chuck has written numerous books and booklets on many subjects.

Based on the outlines and transcripts of Chuck's sermons, the study guide text is co-authored by Bryce Klabunde, a graduate of Biola University and Dallas Theological Seminary. He also wrote the Living Insights sections.

Editor in Chief:
Cynthia Swindoll

Coauthor of Text:
Bryce Klabunde

Assistant Editor:
Wendy Peterson

Copy Editor:
Deborah Gibbs

Text Designer:
Gary Lett

Publishing System Specialist:
Bob Haskins

Director, Communications Division:
Deedee Snyder

Marketing Manager:
Alene Cooper

Project Coordinator:
Colette Muse

Production Manager:
John Norton

Printer:
Sinclair Printing Company

Unless otherwise identified, all Scripture references are from the New American Standard Bible, © The Lockman Foundation 1960, 1962, 1963, 1968, 1971, 1972, 1973, 1975, 1977. Used by permission. The other translations cited are the *Berkeley Version in Modern English* [BV], *The Living Bible* [LB], and *The New Testament in Modern English* [PHILLIPS].

CONTENTS

INTRODUCTION

I got the initial idea for this series while at a nearby college track. I had finished my run and decided to take a closer look at one of the high hurdles on the side of the track. Standing next to one of those things gave me a new respect for the athletes who call themselves hurdlers. Raised to a height of three feet, six inches, the hurdle comes almost to my waist. If you don't think that's high, try jumping one (when no one's looking)! Then imagine running as fast as you can and leaping over ten in a row, spaced about three strides apart. Remarkable!

I used to look critically at runners who would knock over a hurdle or two during a race. Not anymore. I'm amazed that they are able to clear *any* of them.

In the race God has set before each of us, we also face hurdles. High ones, like suffering, reluctance, lukewarmness, confusion. These, and many others, rise up like intimidating obstacles on the track, hindering our obedience to God's call. How can we clear them without tumbling headlong into the dirt?

God's Word, along with the Spirit's empowering presence, gives us the boost we need to overcome these obstacles. The hurdles may seem too high to clear, but God is higher still. He can work through us to make it happen as He brings us to the finish line.

Chuck Swindoll

Chuck Swindoll

PUTTING TRUTH
INTO ACTION

K nowledge apart from application falls short of God's desire for
His children. He wants us to apply what we learn so that we
will change and grow. This study guide was prepared with these
goals in mind. As you go through the following pages, we hope your
desire to discover biblical truth will grow as your understanding of
God's Word increases and that you will be encouraged to apply what
you've learned.

To assist you in your study, we've included a section called
Living Insights at the end of each lesson. These exercises will
challenge you to study further and to think of specific ways to put
your discoveries into action.

There are many ways to use this guide—in personal devotions,
group studies, discussions with friends and family, and Sunday school
classes. And, of course, it's an ideal study aid when you're listening
to its corresponding *Insight for Living* radio series.

To benefit most from this study guide, we would encourage you
to consider it a spiritual journal. That's why we've included space
in the **Living Insights** for recording your thoughts and discoveries.
We hope you'll return to those sections often for review and encouragement as you continue to grow in your walk with Christ.

Bryce Klabunde

Bryce Klabunde
Coauthor of Text
Author of Living Insights

CLEARING
THE HIGH
HURDLES

OVERCOMING OBSTACLES TO OBEYING GOD'S CALL

Chapter 1

CLEARING THE HURDLE OF UNPREPAREDNESS

Matthew 25:1–13

The night before the wedding, Glenda had a terrible time falling asleep. Anticipation had blended with anxiety to brew a strong pot of emotional coffee from which she had been drinking all day. Now she lay in bed, staring wide-eyed into the darkness. Her thoughts spun like a merry-go-round. Images of family and friends and, of course, Steve whirled by in a blur—accompanied by a ranging flock of fears. *What was Aunt So-and-so's name again? Oh, I'll never remember everybody. Where did I put my makeup bag? I just know I'm going to trip over my dress.* All this thinking left her exhausted. At 2 A.M. she finally passed through the door of a fitful, apprehensive sleep.

To her distress, however, her anxieties fluttered right behind.

In a dream, she found herself standing at the back of the church, her heart pounding with excitement. This was her moment to shine—a little girl's fairy tale come true. The church was packed. As the organ trumpeted her cue, every head turned, and she slowly glided down the aisle, blushing and smiling. At the front of the church stood her Steve, handsome and calm and . . . snickering.

Steve! . . . She looked around; it wasn't just him. Everyone was giggling. *What are they laughing at?* She looked down. *Oh no!* Instead of satin shoes and a flowing white gown, she was wearing pink fluffy slippers and flannel pajamas!

Nooooo!

Her scream jerked her awake, and she sat up in bed with a start, gasping for breath. She blinked and found, to her relief, the childhood dolls and familiar furniture of her bedroom. "What time is it?" she said out loud, lunging for the clock. "Whew, 7 A.M. Plenty of time to get dressed."

Have you ever had a nightmare like Glenda's? The thought of

1

being caught unprepared for an important event gives all of us night sweats. Can you imagine, though, the panic of not being ready for the most significant event of all time, the return of Christ? Yet many people aren't ready. Unpreparedness will block them from taking part in the wedding ceremony that Christ has planned when He comes to take His followers to the marriage feast in heaven (see Rev. 19:6-10). It's the first and most crucial hurdle everyone must clear in the spiritual race—the hurdle that Jesus talks about in a parable in Matthew 25.

Background: A Wedding in Palestine

To understand the truths in Jesus' parable, it's important to review the ancient Palestinian wedding customs, which differ from ours today on several points. The following chart contrasts some of these customs.

Wedding Customs in Our Day	Wedding Customs in Jesus' Day
The bride receives the glory and attention.	The groom received the glory and attention.
The bride's parents shoulder the financial load.	The groom or the groom's parents picked up the tab.
The man and woman meet, fall in love, get engaged, and plan their wedding.	The couple had little say about the arrangement of the marriage.

On their way to the altar, a Palestinian couple passed through four stages.

The Engagement. While they were still children, their fathers would arrange their marriage as if they were negotiating a business deal. Romance had nothing to do with the selection. In those days, it was marriage first, then love.

The Betrothal. When the children reached marriageable age, between 12 and 18, a betrothal document was drawn up and signed. It included an agreement concerning the dowries and gifts that the families would exchange. The contract was so binding, it could only be broken by death or divorce.

The Ceremony. About a year later came the wedding day. Dressed like a prince, the bridegroom would lead his attendants at night to the bride's house, where she would be waiting for him in all her glory. Lending to the festivity was the fact that the bride

2

did not know exactly when he would appear. Finally arriving with great fanfare, the groom would escort his bejeweled princess through the city streets back to his house for the ceremony.[1] Lit up by torches and accompanied by singers and dancers, the wedding procession was a spectacular event. Neighbors along the route would drape themselves out windows to watch and cheer as the parade passed by.

The Celebration. The wedding feast followed, sometimes lasting seven to fourteen days. No rushing off to Niagara Falls for these honeymooners. Treated like royalty, they would stay and enjoy the celebration in their honor.

Parable: A Story about Being Prepared

Out of this trousseau of traditions, Jesus draws a powerful parallel, illustrating an important truth about His second coming and the future "kingdom of heaven."

The Underlying Subject

"Then the kingdom of heaven will be comparable to ten virgins, who took their lamps, and went out to meet the bridegroom." (Matt. 25:1)

Christ is the bridegroom, who will return to earth at any moment to escort His beloved ones to heaven. The ten virgins represent those who know that He is coming. Some of them carefully prepare for His arrival; others, tragically, fail to plan ahead.[2]

Bridesmaids, Lamps, and Oil

"And five of them were foolish, and five were prudent. For when the foolish took their lamps, they took no oil with them, but the prudent took oil in flasks along with their lamps." (vv. 2–4)

---

1. G. Christian Weiss describes two processions. Earlier in the evening, the bride would lead an entourage of bridesmaids to the groom's house, where she would wait for her husband-to-be. Later that night, the groom's torch-lit procession would arrive at the house and would be welcomed by the bride's attendants and ushered in for the ceremony and feast. *Insights into Bible Times and Customs* (Chicago, Ill.: Moody Press, 1972), pp. 86–89.

2. Some commentators find a spiritual meaning for every element of the parable—the bride is the church, the surprise arrival is the Rapture, and so on. While we acknowledge their wisdom in this, we have chosen a more general approach, emphasizing the central message of the parable, which is a call to be ready for the coming of Christ, whenever that may be.

Why didn't the foolish virgins bring oil? Perhaps they didn't want to mess with it, or maybe they figured someone else would give them what they needed. Possibly they thought, *I don't feel like worrying about oil right now. Let's just go.* They were like eager children rushing out to play in the snow without their coats and mittens—they simply didn't think ahead. In time, however, they would wish they had.

Jesus continues,

> "Now while the bridegroom was delaying, they all got drowsy and began to sleep. But at midnight there was a shout, 'Behold, the bridegroom! Come out to meet him.' Then all those virgins rose, and trimmed their lamps. And the foolish said to the prudent, 'Give us some of your oil, for our lamps are going out.' But the prudent answered, saying, 'No, there will not be enough for us and you too; go instead to the dealers and buy some for yourselves.'" (vv. 5–9)

So the five foolish girls race around town in a panic, banging on oil merchants' doors until one of them sells them some oil. Flasks in hand, they hurry back. However,

> "while they were going away to make the purchase, the bridegroom came, and those who were ready went in with him to the wedding feast, and the door was shut." (v. 10)

Out of breath, the bridesmaids frantically knock on the door, calling, "Lord, lord, open up for us" (v. 11). But it is too late. The groom answers, "Truly I say to you, I do not know you" (v. 12).

Warning and Reason

As the cries of the foolish bridesmaids fade, Jesus brings the lesson home with a warning,

> "Be on the alert then, for you do not know the day nor the hour."

A person "on the alert" is a person who is always ready—like fire fighters waiting in the station house. They sleep, eat, talk, do their jobs, play games . . . but always they are aware that the alarm may ring at any moment: "Behold, Christ, the Bridegroom! Come out to meet Him!" We must be ready.

It's not enough to know the Bridegroom's name, or even to acknowledge that He's coming. The foolish virgins knew that much. They were turned away, not because they fell asleep or weren't sincere. They were left out because they weren't prepared when the bridegroom came. The example of the prudent gave them plenty of warning that they needed oil. Yet they willfully neglected to make preparations when they had the chance.

Relevance: What about Us Today?

So the lesson of the story is . . . always keep a flask of oil handy, because you never know when a bridegroom will need a lamp. Well, not exactly. Jesus wasn't concerned so much about us having oil in our lamps as having faith in our hearts. Our salvation is the central issue in this parable. Are we spiritually prepared to face Christ if He were to return today? The story teaches four life-or-death principles.

First, *preparation is an individual responsibility.* God doesn't offer us soul insurance on a "group" plan. Just as the foolish virgins were each responsible for their own lamps, so we are responsible for our own hearts.

Second, *no warning precedes Christ's arrival.* The waiting virgins heard the shout, "Behold, the bridegroom," but by then it was too late. Throughout history, people have tried to shout an early warning and predict the date of Christ's return, but Jesus Himself confides,

> "Of that day and hour no one knows, not even the angels of heaven, nor the Son, but the Father alone." (24:36)

Like the devastating flood in Noah's time, the end will take everyone by surprise. People will be "eating and drinking," "marrying and giving in marriage"—consumed with everyday concerns (vv. 37–39). Then, without warning, heavenly trumpets will sound, and Christ will break through the clouds, raining judgment upon the world.

Third, *there is no alternative if you are not ready.* Just as the foolish virgins couldn't borrow oil to make up for their lack of readiness, so we can't slip into the celebration on the coattails of a friend or a relative. People count on all kinds of things to open the door to the feast for them—their moral reputation, their church affiliation, their charitable deeds. But all invitations are examined individually, and only those signed with the blood of the Lamb can gain us entrance. How can you obtain that signature on your heart? The apostle Paul makes it simple.

> If you confess with your mouth Jesus as Lord, and believe in your heart that God raised Him from the dead, you shall be saved. (Rom. 10:9)

Fourth, *the time to prepare is now.* Have you trusted Christ for your salvation? God is calling you to be saved (2 Pet. 3:9). Obeying His call and clearing the hurdle of spiritual unpreparedness is life's primary task. Nothing else is more important. Perhaps you have attended church for many years; you have sung the hymns and listened to the sermons; you have joined hands with those who are awaiting Christ's return—but you have never made Christ your own. Don't put off the decision. Tell Him you believe in Him right now, and begin to live in the light of His truth.

 *Living Insights*

God has made it as simple as possible to be prepared for eternity. A step of faith, that's all—and we've cleared the hurdle. Fear and doubt, however, have filled many a shoe with lead.

What will people think of me? Can I really trust Him? I have clung to my treasures for so long; what if He asks me to give them up?

These thoughts weigh us down so heavily that it seems impossible to budge. But, all that we need do is cry out to Jesus in the words of one distressed father, "I do believe; help my unbelief" (Mark 9:24). And that is all the prompting He needs to leave the courts of heaven, fly to our side, and help us over the obstacle.

Prior to His crucifixion, Jesus proclaimed, "And I, if I be lifted up from the earth, will draw all men to Myself" (John 12:32). Have you been feeling His divine tug? Are you ready to take the step of faith, however small it may be?

If your answer is yes, perhaps this simple prayer can guide your response:

> *Dear Jesus:*
> *You know that I'm a sinner. You shed Your blood on the cross and died to provide me a way to have eternal life with You. I believe in You. I believe that God has*

forgiven my sins because of what You've done for me. With Your help, I step over whatever hurdle might be keeping me from Your side. You are my only way to salvation. Thank You for receiving me into Your kingdom. Amen.

If you entered Christ's kingdom just now, won't you write us and tell us about it? We have a staff of counselors who would love to encourage you in your new journey with the Lord. Write to: Insight for Living, Counseling Department, Post Office Box 69000, Anaheim, California 92817-0900.

Chapter 2

CLEARING THE HURDLE OF SUFFERING

Selected Scriptures

If you could choose your life's course, which one would you choose—the rocky course or the smooth? Silly question, huh? Most people would select the smoothest path—the flower-lined lane filled with an assortment of sights, smells, and pleasurable diversions. It would be a well-manicured trail. No chuckholes, no jagged rocks, and no steep hills to climb. Only soft grass to soothe the feet and soft winds to cool the brow.

The easygoing, problem-free life sounds inviting, doesn't it? No worries about money . . . no hassles with the kids . . . no headaches at work . . . no skirmishes with the neighbors—no stress, no friction, no pain.

Unfortunately, no such course exists. Standing like iron barriers in everyone's path are hurdles of suffering—severe impediments that cut and bruise and send us sprawling in the dirt. We can't remove the difficulties or the pain, but we can learn the lessons those experiences teach, and those are often the most valuable lessons of all.

Lessons Taught Severely

Can anything valuable come from suffering? Malcolm Muggeridge, a highly respected political writer who turned to Christ late in life, once said that, for him, the rockiest roads were the richest.

> Contrary to what might be expected, I look back on experiences that at the time seemed especially desolating and painful with particular satisfaction. Indeed, I can say with complete truthfulness that everything I have learned in my seventy-five years in this world, everything that has truly enhanced and enlightened my existence, has been through affliction and not through happiness, whether pursued or attained. In other words, if it ever were to be possible to eliminate affliction from our earthly existence by means of some drug or other medical

8

mumbo jumbo . . . the result would not be to make life delectable, but to make it too banal and trivial to be endurable. This, of course, is what the Cross signifies. And it is the Cross, more than anything else, that has called me inexorably to Christ.[1]

There are many aspects of Christ we can't identify with. Our words aren't infallible like His; our works aren't miraculous; our character isn't perfect. But our mutual pain links our hearts with His on a deeply human level. Think of His passion—Jesus was betrayed, beaten, spit upon, rejected, cursed, and killed. Jesus knows the searing heat of the crucible. When we suffer, He understands.

He also knows the value of the process. The writer to the Hebrews tells us,

> Although He was a Son, He learned obedience from the things which He suffered. (5:8)

The all-knowing Son of God *learned* something? How can that be?

Christ has always submitted to the Father in perfect obedience, but He did not know what it was like to obey to the point of suffering. Before He became a man, He had never felt pain. It was a new experience for Him—and a necessary one, if He was going to mediate between us and God as our high priest.

Because of His incarnation, He can see suffering through our eyes.

> For we do not have a high priest who cannot sympathize with our weaknesses, but one who has been tempted in all things as we are, yet without sin. Let us therefore draw near with confidence to the throne of grace, that we may receive mercy and may find grace to help in time of need. (vv. 15–16)

Jesus has run the full distance in the human race, through death and beyond. And He's waiting at the finish line, calling to us, "Keep going. I've made it across the highest hurdles of suffering, and I'm here to encourage you every step of the way."

Some Christians think (or are led to believe) that Jesus will remove all their hurdles when they become His followers. He doesn't. He leaves them in our paths—but not because He delights in seeing us stumble. Like any loving father, He weeps for our pain

---

1. Malcolm Muggeridge, *A Twentieth-Century Testimony* (Nashville, Tenn.: Thomas Nelson Publishers, 1978), n.p.

and failure and disappointment; yet He knows that without it, we will never mature. Suffering never feels good, but it can produce good in us. The psalmist wrote,

> It is good for me that I was afflicted,
> That I may learn Thy statutes. (Ps. 119:71)

Affliction makes our hearts tender, drawing us closer to God. It cultivates in us the beautiful rose of obedience . . . the same rose that bloomed in Christ.

Four Experiences, Four Lessons in Obedience

Let's examine four experiences of suffering from Jesus' life that taught Him lessons in obedience. Each one is bound to look familiar, for, in one form or another, we have faced them all.

When Suffering Criticism

Jesus learned obedience through the severity of what people said against Him. In John 8, He encounters His most vicious critics, the Pharisees. The setting is the temple, and Jesus is speaking as they circle Him like a pack of hungry jackals:

> "I know that you are Abraham's offspring; yet you seek to kill Me, because My word has no place in you. I speak the things which I have seen with My Father; therefore you also do the things which you heard from your father." (vv. 37–38)

"Abraham is our father," the Pharisees snap back (v. 39a). But Jesus responds,

> "If you are Abraham's children, do the deeds of Abraham. But as it is, you are seeking to kill Me, a man who has told you the truth, which I heard from God; this Abraham did not do. You are doing the deeds of your father." (vv. 39b–41a)

Their evil intentions exposed, the Pharisees take three verbal swipes at His character. First, they make a vulgar insinuation: "We were not born of fornication"—unlike You (v. 41, emphasis added). Their sources had told them about Mary's hushed pregnancy and quick marriage to Joseph. In their minds, Jesus was an illegitimate child, a sinner by birth.

In verse 48, the Jewish leaders cut Him twice more: "Do we not say rightly that You are a Samaritan and have a demon?" The Samaritans were descendants of Jews and pagan Gentiles, outcasts and half-breeds as far as the Pharisees were concerned. To call Jesus a Samaritan was a sharp jab, but to say that He had a demon . . . that was the ultimate offense to the Son of God.

The mighty angels in heaven must have yearned to teach those scoundrels a lesson in manners. But the only one learning a lesson that day was Jesus. While suffering insults, He did not insult back. He obeyed the Father, even when criticized.

When Suffering Persecution

Jesus also learned obedience through what people *did* against Him. It wasn't long before the verbal slaps turned into active aggression.

After Jesus raised Lazarus from the dead, the Pharisees' murderous desires grew into a detailed plan to get rid of Him (see 11:47–53). As a result, Jesus limited His movement and

> no longer continued to walk publicly among the Jews, but went away from there to the country near the wilderness, into a city called Ephraim; and there He stayed with the disciples. (v. 54)

The religious leaders had issued a warrant for Jesus' arrest. And by the time Passover arrived, they were enlisting informants:

> Now the chief priests and the Pharisees had given orders that if anyone knew where He was, he should report it, that they might seize Him. (v. 57)

Imagine the stress these hostilities must have piled on Jesus' shoulders. He was hunted like a criminal, forced into hiding, and constantly in danger of being turned over to the authorities. But Jesus knew the secret of handling pressure—a secret that missionary Hudson Taylor expressed so well:

> "It doesn't matter, really, how great the pressure is . . . it only matters *where the pressure lies.* See that it never comes *between* you and the Lord—then, the greater the pressure, the more it presses you to His breast."[2]

---

2. Howard and Geraldine Taylor, *Hudson Taylor's Spiritual Secret* (Chicago, Ill.: Moody Press, 1932), Urbana edition, p. 152.

The hounding, the threats, the persecution all pressed Him closer to His Father, welding Him to His Father's will and strengthening His resolve to obey.

When Suffering Silence

The third experience of suffering must have been the worst: He learned obedience when God remained silent. It's distressing to hear ugly things said about you; it's frightening to be chased by persecutors; but nothing can compare to the agony of rushing to God for help and seeing the doors of heaven slam shut in your face. Jesus' anguish in the Garden of Gethsemane reveals what that feels like:

> And He came out and proceeded as was His custom to the Mount of Olives; and the disciples also followed Him. And when He arrived at the place, He said to them, "Pray that you may not enter into temptation." And He withdrew from them about a stone's throw, and He knelt down and began to pray, saying, "Father, if Thou art willing, remove this cup from Me; yet not My will, but Thine be done." Now an angel from heaven appeared to Him, strengthening Him. And being in agony He was praying very fervently; and His sweat became like drops of blood, falling down upon the ground. (Luke 22:39–44)

What sorrow! Where is the "wonderful plan" that God had for Jesus' life? At this moment, the course was rugged and hard to travel. Again and again, Jesus fell against the rocks of God's will, yet He refused to go an easier way. He had learned to follow, even though the One He was following seemed so far away.

When Suffering the Ultimate Wrong

Jesus learned the final lesson of obedience as wrong reached its fulfillment at the Cross. At the crucifixion, all the vulturous evils of hell gathered to feed upon Christ: hatred . . . slander . . . revenge . . . cruelty. He suffered it all. No abused child can cry out without Him feeling the pain. No victim of rape can burn with rage without Him understanding the indignity. Yet the pounding of His afflictions did not crush Him. Why? Because He kept clinging to the Father.

Clearing the Hurdle

If we want to follow Jesus, we must understand from the outset that we are choosing the more difficult course. "In the world you have tribulation," Jesus warned (John 16:33). People will criticize us as they did Jesus. They will hammer their spikes of persecution into our flesh. There will be times when we will languish in the desolate Garden of Gethsemane, when the marshaled evils of this world attack us in full force. The question is, Will our afflictions make us obedient . . . or bitter?

The answer depends on our perspective. The bitter person sees only the loss; the obedient person digs deeper and uncovers the hidden gain. What are suffering's buried treasures? Richer faith. Stronger character. Sweeter fellowship with Christ. Deeper understanding of the Cross. Fuller dependence on God. Only He can take the rough stones of our afflictions and turn them into gold.

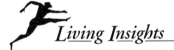

Living Insights

Adversity has the unexpected result of weakening us to the point of dependence on God—where we find our greatest strength! As a result, the things that should tear us down build us up. The heat that should melt our faith tempers it into steel. The furious wind that should topple us sends our roots deeper into Christ.

C. H. Spurgeon, who often suffered fits of depression and bouts with severe illness, said this about the surprising irony of suffering:

> The Christian gains by his losses. He acquires health by his sickness. He wins friends through his bereavements, and he becomes a conqueror through his defeats. Nothing therefore, can be injurious to the Christian, when the very worst things that he has are but rough waves to wash his golden ships home to port and enrich him.[3]

Maybe you're riding out some rough waves right now. Which of Christ's sufferings are you enduring?

___ Criticism

---

3. Charles H. Spurgeon, *Spurgeon at His Best,* comp. Tom Carter (Grand Rapids, Mich.: Baker Book House, 1988), p. 206.

_____ Persecution

_____ Silence

_____ The ultimate cruelties of this world

Besides the trials that Christ endured, have you experienced other kinds of suffering?

_____

_____

_____

How can our study of Christ change your perspective on suffering?

_____

_____

_____

Many people must learn to clear not only the hurdle of suffering but the fear of suffering as well. Has our study helped calm your anxiety about adversity? How so?

_____

_____

_____

What lesson of obedience is God teaching you through your pain?

_____

_____

_____

As you close this chapter, prayerfully meditate on the following verses and, in the space provided, express to the Lord your dependence on His power so that your loss can become gain. We've switched the pronouns to help you make Paul's thoughts your own.

> But *I* have this treasure in earthen vessels, that
> the surpassing greatness of the power may be of God

and not from *myself*; *I* am afflicted in every way, but not crushed; perplexed, but not despairing; persecuted, but not forsaken; struck down, but not destroyed; always carrying about in the body the dying of Jesus, that the life of Jesus also may be manifested in *my* body. (2 Cor. 4:7–10, emphasis added)

_____

_____

_____

_____

_____

_____

_____

_____

_____

_____

_____

_____

_____

_____

_____

_____

_____

_____

_____

Chapter 3

CLEARING THE HURDLE
OF RELUCTANCE
The Book of Jonah

Brrrriiinnngggg!

"There's Junior's alarm," his mother thought to herself, "but I don't hear any rustling in his room. I don't know what's gotten into that boy."

A few minutes later, the alarm sounded again. Then again. Junior was punching the snooze button and burrowing himself deeper under the blankets.

Finally, Mother bustled into his room and took charge. "Son, it's time to get up!"

The mound stirred. Two bleary eyes peeked out from under the covers. "Give me three good reasons," a voice mumbled.

"Well," she said, "number one, it's Sunday and you need to get dressed for church." No response. "Number two, you're forty-three years old and you ought to know better." A little twisting under the covers. "And number three, you're the pastor and the people are expecting you!"[1]

What a surprising scene! Aren't pastors supposed to be noted for their willingness and eager spirit (see 1 Pet. 5:2)? How come this one has to be dragged out of bed? In one word, *reluctance*. A hurdle that trips up both pastor and parishioner, young and old in the faith.

Let's face it, of all the jobs that Christ has given His flock, the one we are most sheepish about is sharing His truth. Paul says, "We are ambassadors for Christ" (2 Cor. 5:20); we are His spokespersons, ministers of His gospel. Yet how many of us feel reluctant to speak for Him?

To overcome this obstacle, we'll need to be very honest with ourselves. It may be painful—muscles that have grown rigid will need to be stretched. But with God's help, we can clear this high hurdle, bringing Him new pleasure in the way we run life's race.

---

1. Adapted from *Illustrations Unlimited*, ed. James S. Hewett (Wheaton, Ill.: Tyndale House Publishers, 1988), p. 182.

Reluctance: A Clarification of the Hurdle

Let's warm up by clearly defining what reluctance is and is not.

What It Is Not

Reluctance to share one's faith is not the same as healthy restraint. Being sensitive, using tact, waiting for the appropriate time—these are signs of maturity, not reluctance. No one wants to be harassed and shoved into the kingdom of God as if in a New York subway stop. Unfortunately, that's what overzealous Christians often do to their unbelieving friends. In Paul's words, "They have a zeal for God, but not in accordance with knowledge" (Rom. 10:2).

What It Is

To actually be reluctant means to deliberately resist telling others about God's grace in Christ. It means purposely holding back the Good News when you know God has sent you.

"Sending," in God's plan, is the foundational step in redeeming humankind. Paul makes that clear in Romans 10:13–15.

> "Whoever will call upon the name of the Lord will be saved." How then shall they call upon Him in whom they have not believed? And how shall they believe in Him whom they have not heard? And how shall they hear without a preacher? And how shall they preach unless they are sent? Just as it is written, "How beautiful are the feet of those who bring glad tidings of good things!"

The following diagram illustrates the stair-step progression in these verses—from God sending us to tell people about Christ to their final response of calling on Him for salvation.

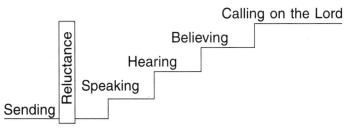

Notice where the hurdle of reluctance stands: right between God's sending and our speaking. The moment we are born into His

17

family, God begins the process of pushing us out of the nest and sending us into the world. The problem is, we're reluctant to spread our wings and fly. We'd rather roost than soar.

To understand one of the reasons for our hesitancy, let's look at the Old Testament prophet most famous for stumbling over the hurdle of reluctance—Jonah.

Jonah: A Prophet Who Resisted the Command

As Jonah's story begins, we hear God's voice sounding strong and clear, like a starter's pistol at the beginning of a race.

The Man and His Mission

> The word of the Lord came to Jonah the son of Amittai saying, "Arise, go to Nineveh the great city, and cry against it, for their wickedness has come up before Me." (Jon. 1:1–2)

There's no mistaking the source of the revelation—the Lord; no misunderstanding the command—Jonah receives it directly; and no misinterpreting the job, the place to go, or the desperate need— Nineveh is perishing. God has set the course for His star athlete and sends him off with a bang. How does Jonah react?

He sprints in the opposite direction.

The Response and Its Consequence

> But Jonah rose up to flee to Tarshish from the presence of the Lord. So he went down to Joppa, found a ship which was going to Tarshish, paid the fare, and went down into it to go with them to Tarshish from the presence of the Lord. (v. 3)

Nineveh, the capital city of Israel's brutal enemy, Assyria, lies about five hundred miles to the east. Jonah, however, heads to the farthest point west, Tarshish.[2] Tarshish is the place you go when you're running away from the will of God. It's any place where God's voice fades in the distance—a job, a relationship, a sinful indulgence. (See map on the following page.)

2. Tarshish, probably Tartessus in southern Spain, was the westernmost stop on the trade routes of that time, about 2,500 miles from Joppa. John D. Hannah, "Jonah," in *The Bible Knowledge Commentary*, Old Testament edition, ed. John F. Walvoord and Roy B. Zuck (Wheaton, Ill.: Scripture Press Publications, Victor Books, 1985), p. 1465.

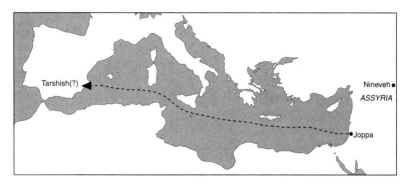

Jonah finds a measure of relief in his rebellion. In the ship's hold, he curls up and falls asleep to the rolling of the waves (v. 5b). He has escaped his troubles and eluded the presence of God . . . or so he thinks.

The psalmist reminds us,

> If I take the wings of the dawn,
> If I dwell in the remotest part of the sea,
> Even there Thy hand will lead me,
> And Thy right hand will lay hold of me.
> (Ps. 139:9–10)

We cannot run from God. He books passages with us on our defiant voyages. And He sends storms our way to change our course toward destruction.

In Jonah's case, the Lord hurls a great wind across the sea, causing the once-restful waves to rear up like lions, pouncing on the ship and nearly tearing it to pieces (Jon. 1:4). Terrified, the pagan sailors cast lots to "learn on whose account this calamity has struck" (v. 7). The lot, of course, falls to Jonah. Bracing themselves against the sea's fury, the sailors plead with him for a way to calm the storm. Over the roar of the wind, Jonah yells back:

> "Pick me up and throw me into the sea. Then the sea will become calm for you, for I know that on account of me this great storm has come upon you." (v. 12)

Jonah's sin has stirred up a storm that crashes on everyone around him. Despite the wreckage his disobedience has caused, though, he refuses to repent. He'd rather die in the murky depths than go to Nineveh.

Not wanting to take Jonah's life, the sailors hesitate. The angry sea growls in response and becomes even stormier. With no alternative, the pagan seamen commit their fates to God and pitch Jonah overboard. Immediately, the ravenous waves are satisfied, and the raging sea calms (vv. 13–15).

The Lord, who hurled the great wind, now summons a great messenger of mercy to snatch up Jonah—a huge fish. In the cold, dark tomb of the fish's stomach, Jonah finally comes to life. The prodigal prophet remembers his heavenly Father and reaches out for His grace. He proclaims:

> "That which I have vowed I will pay.
> Salvation is from the Lord." (2:9b)

He will keep his vow as a prophet to speak for God anywhere, to anybody, at any time. Only after Jonah submits to God does the fish spit him onto dry land—the first amphibious landing!

Repeated Command . . . Reluctant Obedience

After surviving a savage sea and three days of sloshing around in a fish's stomach, Jonah is a mess. But his heart is right. And the word of the Lord comes to him a second time, saying,

> "Arise, go to Nineveh the great city and proclaim to
> it the proclamation which I am going to tell you." (3:2)

His hand always willing to extend a second chance, God points Jonah back to Nineveh. This time, the prophet bolts out of the blocks and swiftly hurdles his reluctance. The rest of the "Romans 10" stair-step progression falls right in place. Jonah speaks God's message (v. 4), the Ninevites believe (v. 5), they call out to God (vv. 6–9), and God saves them.

> When God saw their deeds, that they turned
> from their wicked way, then God relented concern-
> ing the calamity which He had declared He would
> bring upon them. And He did not do it. (v. 10)

All's well that ends well . . . but wait. The story isn't over yet.

Pouting Prophet . . . Gracious God

Nineveh's tears of repentance melt the heart of God, but surprisingly, they fuel the anger of Jonah.

But it greatly displeased Jonah, and he became angry. And he prayed to the Lord and said, "Please Lord, was not this what I said while I was still in my own country? Therefore, in order to forestall this I fled to Tarshish, for I knew that Thou art a gracious and compassionate God, slow to anger and abundant in lovingkindness, and one who relents concerning calamity. Therefore now, O Lord, please take my life from me, for death is better to me than life." And the Lord said, "Do you have good reason to be angry?" (4:1–4)

Jonah thinks he has a good reason. The Ninevites are Israel's enemies—their swords are still red with the blood of the Hebrews. Jonah blew into town like an avenging tornado, a small preview of the wrath to come. But instead of fire and brimstone, the skies rained love and compassion. The patriotic prophet had feared God might pull a switch like this. That's why he had been reluctant to come in the first place.

Like Jonah, we sometimes reinforce our reluctance to speak for God with the bricks of prejudice and hate, and we hold it all together with the mortar of pride. We tend to think only of ourselves. Of our discomfort when we're around people of a different culture. Of our right to take revenge on our enemies. Of our zeal for sinners to be judged.

God, however, wants us to see people the way He sees them. The book of Jonah ends with God's haunting question:

"And should I not have compassion on Nineveh, the great city in which there are more than 120,000 persons who do not know the difference between their right and left hand, as well as many animals?" (v. 11)

Today: A Mandate to Reach Our World

Standing with Jonah atop the high hill of prejudice, we can view ourselves as the righteous "us" and the Ninevites of our world as the ungodly "them"—faceless, nameless people we can categorize by color, politics, and sins. They become the "frightening masses." The "enemy."

As long as we remain up there, feelings of reluctance will continue to get in the way of our mission to preach Christ and make disciples (see Matt. 28:19–20).

To hurdle our reluctance, we must follow Christ to another hill—Mount Calvary. There we view the world through His eyes of love. We see people as individuals, hurting and needy, many of whom are like spiritual children, not knowing their right hand from their left.

Fulfilling our mission as Christ's ambassadors doesn't begin with our going to a foreign land to preach to the nationals. Neither does it begin with our going across the street to witness to a friend. Nor with our dropping a few extra dollars in the missionary's offering basket. It starts in our hearts, where attitudes of smug indifference and pride must be uprooted. That's where the challenge to clear the hurdle of reluctance is met . . . and overcome.

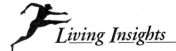

Living Insights

To see the world clearly, we need more than good eyesight. We need good *heart*sight.

The eyes of Jonah's heart had become nearsighted—he cared only for himself and his own people. Thomas John Carlisle's poem "Intercession" points to the cause of Jonah's myopia.

> Abraham interceded for Sodom
> but Jonah couldn't have cared less
> if Nineveh had harbored one
> relatively innocent inhabitant
> or even one hundred and twenty.
> They all looked alike to him—
> seeing he hadn't tried to see them.
> But God's vision is better than twenty-twenty.[3]

Indifference, and even hatred, had blurred Jonah's vision so that he couldn't see the Ninevites as God saw them. He knew God's words well enough, but he didn't know God's heart.

Does God need to check your heart's vision? Who are your "Ninevites"—enemies you would rather see judged than saved? They may be people of a different race, religion, political perspective, or

---

3. Thomas John Carlisle, "Intercession," in *You! Jonah!* (Grand Rapids, Mich.: William B. Eerdmans Publishing Co., 1968), p. 35.

moral lifestyle. They may be your neighbors or even members of your family.

_____

_____

For a few moments, look at your "Ninevites" through the spectacles of Scripture. What do these verses say about God's heart toward the people of the world?

Ezekiel 33:11 _God takes no pleasure in the death_
of wicked people He wants everyone to turn to Him

1 Timothy 1:15 _Christ came to this world to_
save sinners

2:1–6 _God wants everyone to be saved +_
come to a knowledge of Him

In what way do you need to align your vision with God's twenty-twenty standard of mercy?

_____

_____

Coming Around

And Jonah stalked
to his shaded seat
and waited for God
to come around
to his way of thinking.

And God is still waiting
for a host of Jonahs
in their comfortable houses
to come around
to His way of loving.[4]

4. Carlisle, "Coming Around," p. 64.

Chapter 4

CLEARING THE HURDLE OF COMPARISON
John 21:15–22

The instant the starting pistol fires, world-class hurdler Colin Jackson shoots out of the blocks. Nearing the first high hurdle, he kicks up one leg and lunges forward, shaping his body into a lightning bolt. In a flash, he streaks over the barricade and strides for the next. Three steps, hurdle; three steps, hurdle; three steps, hurdle . . . he must clear ten hurdles in all before breaking the tape. And he does so, incredibly, in less than thirteen seconds.

To Colin Jackson, the three-foot-six-inch "high hurdles" are mere speed bumps. To us, they are towering obstacles, much like the hurdles we face every day. What we wouldn't give for his agility as we try to clear the impediments in our path: fear . . . self-doubt . . . pride . . . comparison. That last one has been tripping up God's runners since Peter's day, when the apostle took a running leap and fell face first. Poor Peter—yet who can't identify with his ups and downs?

High Hurdles Familiar to All

As we thumb through the Gospels, we see Peter clearing one hurdle only to fall headlong into the next. He leaps out of the boat to walk on the water with Jesus; then he starts sinking when he looks at the perilous waves (Matt. 14:22–33). He confesses Jesus as the Son of God; then, the next moment, he rebukes Him for predicting His own death (16:13–23). He boasts that he will die with Jesus; then he denies Him later that same night (Luke 22:33–34, 54–62).

In matters of faith, Peter is a world-class stumbler. He's impulsive, temperamental, and reckless . . . just like us! That's why we like him. We see ourselves in his inconsistencies.

But take heart. Despite Peter's stumbling, Jesus never gave up on him. He knew this wavering reed would eventually become the solid rock upon which the church would be built. In Acts we see Peter become a pillar of faith, preaching to thousands and testifying before the same rulers who crucified Jesus.

Before Peter was mightily used in Acts, though, he had one crucial obstacle to clear. It's recorded in John 21; and although we're familiar with the chapter, we often fail to notice this particular hurdle. This obstacle is a dangerous one we tend to ignore—the hurdle of comparison.

One Hurdle We Tend to Ignore

"It's the Lord!" John shouted.

Of course, thought Peter. Who else but Jesus, in just a few seconds, could stuff their nets full of fish after they had spent all night dragging the depths in vain. He had done it before, three years ago—the last time Peter went fishing (Luke 5:1–11).

Why hadn't Peter recognized the voice that shouted from the shore, "Cast the net on the right side of the boat" (John 21:6)? Maybe because he didn't want to. Maybe the shame of his denial still hung heavy in his heart. But Jesus was here; He had come back. Not about to let this opportunity slip away, Peter flung himself into the water and swam ahead of the boat toward Jesus.

As the sun rose over the Sea of Galilee, Peter and a few other disciples gathered around a smoldering fire on the shore. The smell of broiled fish filled the air. It was a breakfast none of them, especially Peter, would ever forget.

A Searching Question Asked Three Times

So when they had finished breakfast, Jesus said to Simon Peter, "Simon, son of John, do you love Me more than these?" He said to Him, "Yes, Lord; You know that I love You." He said to him, "Tend My lambs." He said to him again a second time, "Simon, son of John, do you love Me?" He said to Him, "Yes, Lord; You know that I love You." He said to him, "Shepherd My sheep." He said to him the third time, "Simon, son of John, do you love Me?" Peter was grieved because He said to him the third time, "Do you love Me?" And he said to Him, "Lord, You know all things; You know that I love You." Jesus said to him, "Tend My sheep." (vv. 15–17)

Jesus asks the same question three times—once for each time

Peter denied Him.[1] No doubt, Peter's failure had put a question mark in the minds of the disciples about his competence as a leader. Jesus' words were not meant to heap further shame on His number-one soldier, but to restore him in front of his peers.

After each question, Jesus commissions Peter to immediate service: "Tend My lambs," "Shepherd My sheep," "Tend My sheep." Notice, He doesn't say, "Now, Peter. You said you loved Me before, and we all know what happened. I'm putting you on probation until you've proven your love." No, He takes Peter at his word, reinstates him to full rank, and entrusts him with caring for His followers.

Peter, meanwhile, might have wondered about the specifics of this call. What exactly did the Lord mean by "Tend My sheep"? Where and how would he do this? Before His disciple gets tangled up in these secondary issues, Jesus wants him to settle a more basic matter in his relationship with Him.

A Direct Command Stated Once

In verses 18–19, Jesus paints a grim picture of Peter's future, which many see as a prediction of his martyr's death in Rome.[2]

> "Truly, truly, I say to you, when you were younger, you used to gird yourself, and walk wherever you wished; but when you grow old, you will stretch out your hands, and someone else will gird you, and bring you where you do not wish to go." Now this He said, signifying by what kind of death he would glorify God. (vv. 18–19a)

Then He confronts him with a direct challenge:

> And when He had spoken this, He said to him, "Follow Me!" (v. 19b)

The Greek tense suggests that Jesus is saying, "Follow and *keep on* following Me!" This is the key issue in discipleship: Are we

---

1. In His first two questions, Jesus uses the Greek word for the highest form of love, *agapaō*—God's sacrificial love. Peter knows his failure-prone heart and can only answer using the Greek word for brotherly love, *phileō*. In His third question, Jesus changes from *agapaō* to *phileō*, recognizing the weaknesses in Peter's life.

2. "[Peter] will serve into old age and in the end die with hands outstretched, a euphemism for crucifixion. The details are not known with certainty, but there is fairly reliable tradition that Peter followed his Lord in the form of his death, probably in Rome under the Emperor Nero in the early sixties of the first century." Bruce Milne, *The Message of John: Here Is Your King!*, The Bible Speaks Today Series (Downers Grove, Ill.: InterVarsity Press, 1993), p. 318.

willing to surrender our wills to Christ and to keep on following Him through hardships, persecution, and even death?

A Reluctant Response Quietly Asked

Just as he did after Jesus' initial challenge three years before (see Mark 1:16–18), Peter immediately leaves his nets and follows his Lord. Not two steps into his restored relationship with Christ, however, he stumbles over the obstacle of comparison.

> Peter, turning around, saw the disciple whom Jesus loved following them; the one who also had leaned back on His breast at the supper, and said, "Lord, who is the one who betrays You?" Peter therefore seeing him said to Jesus, "Lord, and what about this man?" (John 21:20–21)

Why does Peter suddenly look back now? Unlike Lot's wife, he's not pining for worldly treasures. He's simply curious about his friend. *I wonder what John's future is?* And curiosity can quickly swirl into a whirlpool of comparison. *Will he die a martyr's death like me? Is Christ asking me to sacrifice more than He's asking John?*

With thoughts like these probably churning in his mind, Peter turns from the Lord to look at John. Ah, Peter, Peter. Will he ever learn to fix his eyes on Christ and keep them there?

Will we?

A Strong Reply Forcefully Expressed

In verse 22, Jesus reminds Peter of where his focus needs to be.

> Jesus said to him, "If I want him to remain until I come, what is that to you? You follow Me!"

The Savior says to the curious disciple, in so many words, "Mind your own business! John is not your concern." Then He says, literally, "You, Me, keep on following."

Let's Think about That Hurdle, Then Clear It!

Few obstacles in the Christian race sideline us with twisted ankles faster than comparison. Like Peter, we start well, proclaiming our love for the Lord and our willingness to leave our nets and follow Him. But then, when fulfilling Christ's mission gets tough, curiosity whispers in our ears: "How well is so-and-so doing?" Taking our eyes off the Lord, we start checking out the other runners. (To be honest, we even get a little nosy.)

Thoughts like this enter our minds: *Look at Bill over there. While I've been serving the Lord and making sacrifices, he's been making a killing in business. When am I going to get my share?*

How swiftly curiosity hurls us into comparison and dashes us into gossip . . . envy . . . pride . . . judgmental attitudes . . . and unhappiness in God's calling.

How can we overcome this hazard? Here are a few tips:

1. Admit your tendency to compare yourself with others.

2. Next time you feel the urge to compare, confess it openly. Treat it like it is—a disease that damages your walk with the Lord.

3. Return to the Lord for refreshment. Ask the Lord to show you the blessings and challenges you've begun to lose sight of.

4. Remind yourself that following *Him* is your assignment. Don't be concerned with anyone else's job.

As the writer to the Hebrews summed up,

> Let us strip off everything that hinders us, as well as the sin which dogs our feet, and let us run the race that we have to run with patience, our eyes fixed on Jesus the source and the goal of our faith. (Heb. 12:1b–2a PHILLIPS)

Let's leave the hurdle of comparison in our dust as we stride on to Jesus, who waits with open arms at the finish line.

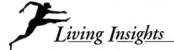

Living Insights

C. S. Lewis, in *The Horse and His Boy* from his Chronicles of Narnia series, illustrates God's perspective on our habit of comparing ourselves to others.

The main character, Shasta, is wandering up a road that has led him high into the cold, misty mountains. Lost and hungry and feeling very sorry for himself, the boy begins to cry, when he suddenly realizes that he is not alone. Through the mist he hears, then feels, the breathing of a large creature. It is the lion Aslan—who asks Shasta to tell him his sorrows.

Shasta was a little reassured by the breath: so he told how he had never known his real father or mother and had been brought up sternly by the fisherman. And then he told the story of his escape and how they were chased by lions and forced to swim for their lives; and of all their dangers in Tashbaan and about his night among the Tombs and how the beasts howled at him out of the desert. And he told about the heat and thirst of their desert journey and how they were almost at their goal when another lion chased them and wounded Aravis. And also how very long it was since he had had anything to eat.

"I do not call you unfortunate," said the Large Voice.

"Don't you think it was bad luck to meet so many lions?" said Shasta.

"There was only one lion," said the Voice.

"What on earth do you mean? I've just told you there were at least two the first night, and—"

"There was only one: but he was swift of foot."

"How do you know?"

"I was the lion." And as Shasta gaped with open mouth and said nothing, the Voice continued. "I was the lion who forced you to join with Aravis. I was the cat who comforted you among the houses of the dead. I was the lion who drove the jackals from you while you slept. I was the lion who gave the Horses the new strength of fear for the last mile so that you should reach King Lune in time. And I was the lion you do not remember who pushed the boat in which you lay, a child near death, so that it came to shore where a man sat, wakeful at midnight, to receive you.

"Then it was you who wounded Aravis?"

"It was I."

"But what for?"

"Child," said the Voice, "I am telling you your story, not hers. I tell no one any story but his own."[3]

3. C. S. Lewis, *The Horse and His Boy* (New York, N.Y.: Macmillan Publishing Co., Collier Books, 1954), pp. 157 59.

How curious we are to know God's ways in other people's lives and to compare stories. Isn't our own story enough to fill our lives with wonder? Why do we yearn to peek into our neighbor's book and poke around in their pages?

Do you tend to compare God's work in your life with His work in the lives of others? What is at the root of this comparison: feelings of envy or pride, judgmental attitudes, or unhappiness in your life's calling?

_____

_____

_____

Comparing can be habit-forming. If it's a problem in your life, review the four steps at the end of the lesson. Go through these steps at the end of the day, for the next month. Then at the end of each week, record your improvement in the space below. Let's see if we can kick this habit together.

Week 1: _____

_____

Week 2: _____

_____

Week 3: _____

_____

Week 4: _____

_____

Chapter 5

CLEARING THE HURDLE
OF RESISTANCE

Exodus 3:1–4:18

Just as ships need rudders, so our families, schools, churches, and businesses need dedicated leaders to pilot us toward godly goals. And just as it takes only one rudder to guide the mightiest ship, so one person fully committed to the Lord can steer the most powerful movements of God. In every generation and in every group, God looks for that person. But He doesn't always find the one He's searching for, as He told the prophet Ezekiel:

> "I searched for a man among them who should build up the wall and stand in the gap before Me for the land, that I should not destroy it; but I found no one." (Ezek. 22:30)

God still seeks stand-in-the-gap individuals who can lead the way in fulfilling His worldwide mission of redemption. Yet He also continues to run into human resistance. Why? Because we often respond to His summons in ways that wind up obstructing His calling rather than clearing a way for it.

Three of the Most Common Reactions to God's Call

"I want you," we hear the Lord say, and our first reaction is usually *intensity*. Sensing the Lord's mighty hand on our lives, we get overzealous and run ahead of His plan. Before we know it, our feet tangle in a string of foolish decisions, and we land flat on our faces.

Brushing ourselves off, we next react with *insecurity*. Self-doubt and anxiety haunt us like ghosts, frightening away what remains of our confidence. Shivering, we retreat to the safety of the crowd.

Insecurity can then lead to dark feelings of *inferiority*. At one time, we believed we had what it takes to be a leader, but our failure keeps replaying in our brains, "I blew it . . . I blew it . . . I really blew it." So when God calls us again, we resist. He should know that leadership is not our gift. Obviously, He's dialed the wrong number.

These reactions describe Moses in a nutshell. Moses was born at a time perilous for Hebrew babies. To preserve his life, his mother set him adrift in the Nile near Pharaoh's daughter, who rescued him and raised him in Egyptian opulence. He definitely had the power and position to become the savior of his people. But he ran ahead of the Lord and rashly murdered an Egyptian taskmaster who was beating a fellow Hebrew. When Pharaoh got wind of his crime, Moses fled for his life to faraway Midian, where he exchanged his kingly scepter for a shepherd's staff (Exod. 2:1–22).

For the next forty years, the only group Moses led was a flock of sheep. Every day, bleating reminders of his failure echoed through the sparse canyons. Insecurity and inferiority whipped his back like the hot desert winds. *I'm a flop. A has-been. I lost my chance to help my people. Don't ask me to go back . . . I'm through being God's leader.*

But God wasn't through with Moses.

Moses: Resistant to Lead

Before the Lord can use him, Moses has to clear perhaps the highest hurdle standing in the way of those who've failed: resistance to trying again. Let's see how God helps Him over this obstacle.

A Man Clearly Called

God's call comes to Moses in an unusual and unmistakable way.

> Now Moses was pasturing the flock of Jethro his father-in-law, the priest of Midian; and he led the flock to the west side of the wilderness, and came to Horeb, the mountain of God. And the angel of the Lord appeared to him in a blazing fire from the midst of a bush; and he looked, and behold, the bush was burning with fire, yet the bush was not consumed. So Moses said, "I must turn aside now, and see this marvelous sight, why the bush is not burned up." When the Lord saw that he turned aside to look, God called to him from the midst of the bush, and said, "Moses, Moses!" And he said, "Here I am." Then He said, "Do not come near here; remove your sandals from your feet, for the place on which you are standing is holy ground." He said also, "I am the God of your father, the God of Abraham, the God of Isaac, and the God of Jacob." Then Moses hid his face, for he was afraid to look at God. (3:1–6)

Speaking through the crackling flames, the Lord reveals His plan to Moses:

> And the Lord said, "I have surely seen the affliction of My people who are in Egypt, and have given heed to their cry because of their taskmasters, for I am aware of their sufferings. So I have come down to deliver them from the power of the Egyptians, and to bring them up from that land to a good and spacious land, to a land flowing with milk and honey, to the place of the Canaanite and the Hittite and the Amorite and the Perizzite and the Hivite and the Jebusite. And now, behold, the cry of the sons of Israel has come to Me; furthermore, I have seen the oppression with which the Egyptians are oppressing them. Therefore, come now, and I will send you to Pharaoh, so that you may bring My people, the sons of Israel, out of Egypt." (vv. 7–10)

The eighty-year-old Moses takes stock of himself, tallies his deficits, and replies, "Who . . . me?"

> But Moses said to God, "Who am I, that I should go to Pharaoh, and that I should bring the sons of Israel out of Egypt?" (v. 11)

But God isn't concerned about what Moses lacks.

> And He said, "Certainly I will be with you, and this shall be the sign to you that it is I who have sent you: when you have brought the people out of Egypt, you shall worship God at this mountain." (v. 12)

Note the confidence God has in Moses: "*when* you have brought the people out of Egypt." How can the Lord be so sure? Because *He* is the deliverer—Moses is merely His instrument.

A Man Reluctant to Obey

Instead of following the Lord like an obedient sheep, Moses bleats four reasons why he can't go back to Egypt.

1. "*I will not have all the answers.*" Moses' first fear is that the Hebrews will test him with theological questions he can't answer. His ignorance will be paraded before the nation, and he will feel like a fool. Shielding his eyes from the bush's blazing light, he trembles.

"Behold, I am going to the sons of Israel, and I shall say to them, 'The God of your fathers has sent me to you.' Now they may say to me, 'What is His name?' What shall I say to them?" (v. 13)

So God tells Moses what to say; and in giving him the right answer, He gives him this reassurance: *You will have all of Me*.

And God said to Moses, "I AM WHO I AM"; and He said, "Thus you shall say to the sons of Israel, 'I AM has sent me to you.'" (v. 14)

God promises that the people will "pay heed" to what he will say (v. 18). They'll know that the Lord is with him.

As fear number one moves to the back of the line, fear number two inches forward.

2. *"I may not have all their respect."* This fear wears a worried expression and wrings its hands, complaining woefully,

"What if they will not believe me, or listen to what I say? For they may say, 'The Lord has not appeared to you.'" (4:1)

Moses shudders at the hypothetical scenes his fear projects. Pictures of his own people ridiculing and rejecting him. Images of wolves ripping apart what remains of his shredded dignity.[1] The Lord, however, shakes Moses out of his nightmare with two startling miracles, reassuring him with the following promise: *You will have all My power*.

And the Lord said to him, "What is that in your hand?" And he said, "A staff." Then He said, "Throw it on the ground." So he threw it on the ground, and it became a serpent; and Moses fled from it. But the Lord said to Moses, "Stretch out your hand and grasp it by its tail"—so he stretched out his hand and caught it, and it became a staff in his hand—"that they may believe that the Lord, the God of their fathers, the God of Abraham, the God of Isaac, and the God of Jacob, has appeared to you." And the

---

1. The criticism from the two Hebrews forty years earlier probably still stung Moses: "Who made you a prince or a judge over us?" (Exod. 2:14b).

Lord furthermore said to him, "Now put your hand into your bosom." So he put his hand into his bosom, and when he took it out, behold, his hand was leprous like snow. Then He said, "Put your hand into your bosom again." So he put his hand into his bosom again; and when he took it out of his bosom, behold, it was restored like the rest of his flesh. (vv. 2–7)

If these signs don't win the allegiance of the Hebrews, the next one will. God tells Moses that when he gets to Egypt, he is to pour water from the Nile on the ground, and it will become blood (vv. 8–9).

These are nickel-and-dime miracles to God—small change compared to the wealth of power He will pour into Moses' pockets. Even so, Moses feels like a penniless pauper.

3. *"I do not have all the ability."* Tending woollies in the wilderness for forty years has made Moses timid about speaking in public, particularly before the sophisticated court of Pharaoh.

> Then Moses said to the Lord, "Please, Lord, I have never been eloquent, neither recently nor in time past, nor since Thou hast spoken to Thy servant; for I am slow of speech and slow of tongue." (v. 10)

"I . . . I . . ." Moses' eyes are on himself and his limitations. In verses 11 and 12, though, the Lord lifts Moses' face toward heaven and reassures him, *You will have all you need.*

> And the Lord said to him, "Who has made man's mouth? Or who makes him dumb or deaf, or seeing or blind? Is it not I, the Lord? Now then go, and I, even I, will be with your mouth, and teach you what you are to say." (vv. 11–12)

The command is straightforward: "Go!" But Moses, cowering, buries his face in the dust and refuses to budge.

4. *"I'm not as qualified as all the others."* Clutching the earth, he sobs,

> "Please, Lord, now send the message by whomever Thou wilt." (v. 13)

The Berkeley translation expresses the desperation in his voice: "O Lord, please send anyone (else)"! By now, Moses' trepidation sounds more like lack of faith . . . and to God feels like a slap in the face.

> Then the anger of the Lord burned against Moses, and He said, "Is there not your brother Aaron the Levite? I know that he speaks fluently. And moreover, behold, he is coming out to meet you; when he sees you, he will be glad in his heart. And you are to speak to him and put the words in his mouth; and I, even I, will be with your mouth and his mouth, and I will teach you what you are to do. Moreover, he shall speak for you to the people; and it shall come about that he shall be as a mouth for you, and you shall be as God to him." (vv. 14–16)

With Aaron to give him a leg up, Moses reluctantly rolls over his hurdle of resistance. He makes it . . . but barely.

A Man Willing to Obey (Finally!)

His faith flabby and hanging over his belt, Moses isn't exactly what you'd call a spiritual dynamo. Notice the weak reason he gives his father-in-law for wanting to return to Egypt.

> Then Moses departed and returned to Jethro his father-in-law, and said to him, "Please, let me go, that I may return to my brethren who are in Egypt, and see if they are still alive." And Jethro said to Moses, "Go in peace." (v. 18)

To see if they were still alive? Pretty feeble faith. But at least Moses went. And the rest is history.

Three Things to Remember When You're Called to Lead

Now, if God could use trembling, stuttering Moses to stand up to Pharaoh and lead the Hebrews out of Egypt, don't you think He could use us to be leaders where we live?

Before shaking your head and saying, "No, no, no. Not me. I'm not a leader," picture yourself as Moses bowing before the burning bush and listen for a moment. Could God be choosing you to stand for Him in your family? In your church? In your community?

If you're feeling the heat of His call, first, *be sure you're hearing God's voice.* Don't do anything until you square what you're feeling with God's Word. Second, *be confident in God's power as you obey.*

Let Him do the delivering; you're just the instrument. Third, _be open to God's will regardless of your inadequacies._ Ask yourself, "Do I really believe that my weakness is greater than God?"

Moses left the bush still ablaze with the presence of God. Who knows, perhaps it's still burning somewhere, waiting for us to come aside and hear His call.

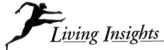
Living Insights

Everybody talks to themselves. Perhaps not out loud, like the transient on the street corner who waves his arms and carries on a heated argument with an invisible companion. Our conversations take place in the hidden chambers of our minds.

For example, what do you say to yourself when you trip in front of a lot of people? _Clumsy! What's your middle name—Grace? That was smooth. Why don't you join the ballet?_

We're our own worst critics. Whether our mistake causes a minor stumble or a major disaster, we continually beat ourselves down with negative self-talk. No wonder when God calls us to do great things for Him, we resist. "I can't," we tell the burning bush. "I'm clumsy. I'm stupid. I'm shy. I'm incapable. I'm ugly."

Listening to us put ourselves down, the Lord probably wants to cover His ears and scream, "Stop it! It's not true!" Read what He thinks of you in the following verses, and finish the statement, "God says that, in Christ, I am . . ."

2 Corinthians 5:17—I am _____

_____

Galatians 3:26—I am _____

_____

Ephesians 2:10—I am_____

_____

Colossians 2:13—I am _____

_____

1 Peter 2:4–5—I am _____

_____

1 Peter 2:9—I am _____

_____

Do you believe what God says about you? If you sometimes doubt His Word, when is it hardest to accept?

When we don't want to leave our comfort
zone. When we feel we can't do something
God wants us to do, we're not qualified or
we might fail

_____

Moses' biggest problem wasn't his lack of skills; it was his lack of faith. It's one thing to acknowledge our weaknesses, but it's another to let those weaknesses become more powerful than God. Read 2 Corinthians 12:5–10. What was Paul's attitude toward his short-comings? Does your confidence rest in the same place Paul's did?

_____

_____

_____

_____

_____

_____

_____

_____

Chapter 6

CLEARING THE HURDLE
OF LUKEWARMNESS

Revelation 3:14–20

The primary task of the local church is . . . ? How would you answer that question? Is it preaching the gospel? Caring for the poor?

Actually, the correct answer is more like, "To help people stay hot for God." Maintaining a wholehearted devotion to God is our top priority. Everything else is a spoke on the church's wheel—good and essential, but not the hub.

The phrase "hot for God" may not roll off the scholarly tongues of many theologians, but it is a concept *we* can sink our teeth into. It's the spiritual fervor expressed by the psalmist:

> As the deer pants for the water brooks,
> So my soul pants for Thee, O God.
> My soul thirsts for God, for the living God.
> (Ps. 42:1–2a)

It's the insatiable passion for truth that motivates us to devour God's Word. It's the relentless compassion for the unsaved that sends us into every corner of the world. It's the unstoppable joy within our hearts that overflows in prayer and praise.

Kindling that spiritual heat within people is the business of the church. Unfortunately, many churches have drifted from their primary task. Instead of bringing the water to boil, they let it stagnate. They fall over the same hurdle that tripped up the Laodicean believers—allowing spiritual lukewarmness to seep into the church.

Case Study: A Church That Drifted into Mediocrity

Some background information about the Laodicean believers will help us understand what factors may have caused their faith to cool.

A Little History

Laodicea was located in the Lychus River valley, not far from Colossae. In A.D. 60, a devastating earthquake leveled the city. Paul's letter to the Colossians, written soon after the disaster, expresses his deep concern for them. Paul writes,

> For I want you to know how great a struggle I have
> on your behalf, and for those who are at Laodicea,
> and for all those who have not personally seen my
> face, that their hearts may be encouraged. (Col. 2:1–2a)

Although he never met these believers, he prayed for them and, apparently, corresponded with them. Notice his reference to a Laodicean letter in the closing verses of Colossians:

> Greet the brethren who are in Laodicea and also
> Nympha and the church that is in her house. And
> when this letter is read among you, have it also read
> in the church of the Laodiceans; and you, for your
> part read my letter that is coming from Laodicea.
> And say to Archippus, "Take heed to the ministry
> which you have received in the Lord, that you may
> fulfill it." (4:15–17)

Who was Archippus? Probably, he was the pastor of the church. Paul wisely forewarned him to "take heed to the ministry"—to tend the spiritual fires and keep the church burning for God. You see, Laodicea had a lot going for it and was a strategic base for the spread of the gospel.

- Economically, it was "one of the richest commercial centres of the ancient world," due to its prime location at the juncture of several key trade routes.[1] So wealthy was the city that, after the A.D. 60 earthquake, the citizens refused subsidies from Rome and rebuilt the city out of their own resources.

- Industrially, Laodicea was famous for the beautiful, raven-colored cloth that it manufactured from the glossy, black wool of the local sheep.[2] The people took pride in the clothing they exported around the world.

- Educationally, the city boasted a renowned medical school, where an eye powder was made to treat weak vision.[3]

1. William Barclay, *Letters to the Seven Churches* (1957; reprint, London, England: SCM Press, 1958), p. 109.

2. Barclay, *Letters to the Seven Churches*, p. 112.

3. Barclay, *Letters to the Seven Churches*, p. 113.

Bountiful resources. Worldwide influence. Academic respect. Laodicea was the perfect place to establish a ministry out of which the gospel's flames could ignite the world. Yet, tragically, during the thirty or so years between Paul's Colossian letter and John's Revelation, the church's fire smoldered and died. What went wrong?

An Honest Appraisal

Christ's own words, recorded by John in Revelation 3, provide us several important leads in solving this mystery.

1. *The church's condition.* Verse 14 reveals Jesus as the only qualified investigator of the situation.

> "And to the angel of the church in Laodicea write:
> The Amen, the faithful and true Witness, the
> Beginning of the creation of God, says this."

He is the "Amen"—His words are final. He is the ideal "Witness"—His testimony is impeccably true. He is the "Beginning"— He sees things like no one else can, from the earliest motives and drives. And what He saw happening at the church in Laodicea wasn't good. Listen to His indictment:

> "'I know your deeds, that you are neither cold nor
> hot; I would that you were cold or hot.'"[4] (v. 15)

With Christ, neutrality is not an option. If He is the Son of God, the Savior of the world, the sovereign of the universe, then He deserves our "hot," wholehearted best. Anything less is an insult. From Jesus' point of view, it's better to be icy toward Him and live consistently with our unbelief than to call Him King and live indifferently.

Sadly, after thirty years of ministry, the middle-aged Laodicean believers had settled into a lounge-chair religion. They had become spiritually fat . . . comfortable . . . lazy. And worse, like the voyagers on the posh Titanic, they didn't even realize how desperate their situation was.

Skipping ahead for a moment to verse 17, we discover a startling contrast between what the believers thought of themselves and their true condition.

---

4. "The Greek words are striking," notes John R. W. Stott, "and we are left in no doubt about their meaning. 'Cold' means icy cold and 'hot' means boiling hot. Jesus Christ would prefer us to boil or to freeze, rather than that we should simmer down into a tasteless tepidity." *What Christ Thinks of the Church* (Grand Rapids, Mich.: William B. Eerdmans Publishing Co., 1958), p. 116.

"'You say, "I am rich, and have become wealthy, and have need of nothing," and you do not know that you are wretched and miserable and poor and blind and naked.'"

On paper, the numbers of this wealthy church added up to a successful, self-sufficient ministry. Spiritually, though, the church was skid-row poor.

William Barclay points to the culprit that apparently stole the church's zeal for the Lord: an insidious longing for a respectable, non-invasive religion.

> A decent respectability was all right and even much to be desired, but a religion which was like a fire in a man's bones, and which pervaded every part and corner of his life, was a different thing altogether. There is such a thing as a kind of common-sense religion. The Ten Commandments are doubtless very proper, but when it comes to an enthusiasm which demands that we should love our enemies, and give our goods to the poor, and pray for the people who insult us—that is a very different matter. Laodicaea is condemned because she preferred a respectable morality to a passionate religion.[5]

2. *Christ's evaluation.* How does the Lord feel about this kind of empty relationship with Him? Back to verse 16:

> "'So because you are lukewarm, and neither hot nor cold, I will spit you out of My mouth.'"

A lukewarm attitude turns His stomach. When we talk about the lost more than reach them, when we go through the motions of worship rather than display true zeal, when we deck ourselves with impressive religious phrases rather than live what we believe, we have become like standing water in a drainage ditch—foul, putrid, nauseating. Jesus would rather our hearts be icy mountain streams or boiling hot springs than tepid pools where algae grows and mosquitoes hover.

Advice and Invitation

What a devastating indictment. But Christ quickly follows with

---

5. Barclay, *Letters to the Seven Churches,* pp. 116–17.

three words of advice designed to rebuild the church's faith.

> "'I advise you to buy from Me gold refined by fire,
> that you may become rich, and white garments, that
> you may clothe yourself, and that the shame of your
> nakedness may not be revealed; and eyesalve to
> anoint your eyes, that you may see. Those whom I
> love, I reprove and discipline; be zealous therefore,
> and repent.'" (vv. 18–19)

Although the Laodiceans think they are above need, in God's eyes they are destitute. So first Jesus tells them to invest their lives in the golden character qualities that produce true riches—the kind of qualities that remain after God's refining fire burns away the self-deceiving motivations of the heart.

Although they clothe themselves in their world-famous black cloth, from God's perspective they are naked. So Jesus advises them to take off their self-righteous attitude and put on the white garments of His righteousness.

And although they pioneered a healing powder for the eyes, to God they are helplessly blind. So Jesus commands them to anoint their minds with heavenly salve, which will open their eyes to spiritual truth.

"Be zealous," Christ exhorts them, "and repent." Turn around. Rekindle your fire for God.

No doubt, Jesus' words of discipline stung, as they sting all lukewarm believers today. But divine discipline comes from a loving hand—the same hand that bids us open our hearts to Him.

> "'Behold, I stand at the door and knock; if anyone
> hears My voice and opens the door, I will come in
> to him, and will dine with him, and he with Me.'"
> (v. 20)

We usually offer this verse to unbelievers with an appeal for salvation. Yet it was actually spoken to Christ's own followers whose hearts had grown indifferent to Him.

"There is no cure for lukewarmness," wrote C. H. Spurgeon, "like a good supper with Christ."[6] To feel His sweet, warming fellowship,

---

6. Charles Haddon Spurgeon, *Spurgeon at His Best,* comp. Tom Carter (Grand Rapids, Mich.: Baker Book House, 1988), p. 366.

what must we do? Quiet our religious static and listen for His quiet voice. Open ourselves to Him. Surrender our will to His. He won't pound and yell and force His way in. We must open the door from the inside.

Let's Take This Personally

Right now, while you have a moment of quiet, test your spiritual temperature. Are you lukewarm? Is your talk sounding more impressive than your walk? Are you taking in more than you're giving out? Perhaps you feel like you're merely going through the religious motions and not experiencing the vitality of God's presence.

If you're nodding yes, come to grips with the peril you're in. Hear Christ's soft and constant rapping at the door.

Won't you let Him in?

 *Living Insights*

Lord, Your honesty hurts. Your words are like swords, and You drive them right through me.

Would you prefer that I be dishonest?

No, no. But couldn't You have chosen a gentler image to describe me? "Straying sheep" has a much softer feel to it. Or how about "weedy garden"? Or "leaky ship"?

Can I help how I feel? Cloaking My emotions in socially acceptable words won't help the situation. I know it hurts, but I must tell you the truth.

So it is true. When I am indifferent toward You, or blasé or even cavalier in my attitude, I am like foul-smelling, stagnant ditch water to You. Is that right? And when I offer myself to You, You take one sip of me and get sick to Your stomach. Is that how I sometimes make You feel? I make You want to vomit?

Yes. I'm sorry. It's true.

◆

The truth about ourselves is indeed a bitter pill to swallow. But we must accept God's diagnosis and take His medicine if He is to heal us. Is He revealing any sickening lukewarmness in your attitudes?

◆

Lord, if I disgust You so, why don't You leave me? You must despise me.

You don't know Me very well, do you? I don't despise you.

But You just said that I make You sick. I don't understand.

Your lukewarm offerings may nauseate Me, but I still love you. You are My child, and there is nothing you can do that will drive Me away from you. I'm always here, right outside your door. Longing to come in.

◆

If it has been a while since you've enjoyed some intimate fellowship with Christ, why don't you spend some time right now "dining" with the Savior? Open the door to your heart's home, and usher Him to the seat of honor. Offer Him a banquet of the things you treasure most—your talents, your hopes, your dreams. Choose a passage from His life in one of the gospels, and meditate on His love for you (for example, John 15).

We've provided some space for you to express your devotion to Him. Let Him bring your heart to a boil.

Chapter 7

CLEARING THE HURDLE OF INDIFFERENCE

Selections from Philippians

Three steps beyond the hurdle of lukewarmness stands the hurdle of indifference. The first one tests our passion for God; the second, our passion for the lost.

The two obstacles are closely related. A lukewarm attitude toward God often simmers into an indifferent attitude toward the world. On the other hand, zeal for God tends to ignite a zeal for the unsaved. We start seeing other cultures through God's eyes. We begin to feel His longing for "all men to be saved" (1 Tim. 2:4). We become more willing to step out of our own backyards and catch God's vision of every person in every nation hearing the good news of Christ.

God may not call each of us to become missionaries in a foreign country. But He does call us all to care about those who do not know Christ. One way we can do that is by caring for those whom God *has* sent to be missionaries. In this chapter and the next, we'll look at the supportive relationship between the Philippian believers and the apostle Paul. We'll see how one church cared for this missionary and, through him, changed the world.

Paul and the Philippians: Some General Observations

As Paul sat down to pen his letter to the Philippians, warm feelings poured from his heart onto the parchment.

> I thank my God in all my remembrance of you,
> always offering prayer with joy in my every prayer
> for you all, in view of your participation in the gospel
> from the first day until now. (Phil. 1:3–5)

Why did he thank God and pray for them so earnestly? Because of their *participation* with him in the gospel. From their first meeting onward, the Philippians clasped hands with Paul concerning his message of salvation and his mission to spread the gospel to the world.

Let's travel back to that first meeting, recorded in Acts 16, and trace some of the ties that bound them so closely together.

First Encounter

Luke and Silas accompanied Paul when he came to Philippi, which was "a leading city of the district of Macedonia, a Roman colony" (Acts 16:12). That last phrase tells us a lot about the city. According to William Barclay,

> Wherever they where, these colonies were little fragments of Rome and their pride in Roman citizenship was their dominant characteristic. The Roman language was spoken; Roman dress was worn; Roman customs were observed; their magistrates had Roman titles, and carried out the same ceremonies as were carried out in Rome itself. They were stubbornly and unalterably Roman and would never have dreamt of becoming assimilated to the people amidst whom they were set.[1]

From their gowns to their government, the Philippians had baptized themselves in Roman culture. Paul and his cohorts came preaching a baptism in the name of Jesus. How would the citizens receive this totally new, completely un-Roman religion? Luke's journal gives us the answer:

> And on the Sabbath day we went outside the gate to a riverside, where we were supposing that there would be a place of prayer; and we sat down and began speaking to the women who had assembled. And a certain woman named Lydia, from the city of Thyatira, a seller of purple fabrics, a worshiper of God, was listening; and the Lord opened her heart to respond to the things spoken by Paul. And when she and her household had been baptized, she urged us, saying, "If you have judged me to be faithful to the Lord, come into my house and stay." And she prevailed upon us. (vv. 13–15)

What a welcome! Just as Paul wrote in his letter, from the very first day these new believers demonstrated openness to the gospel—open hearts, open arms, and even an open home.

---

1. William Barclay, *The Letters to the Philippians, Colossians, and Thessalonians*, rev. ed., The Daily Study Bible Series (Philadelphia, Pa.: Westminster Press, 1975), p. 4.

A Developing Relationship

Later, however, dark clouds of trouble billowed over the city when Paul and Silas cast a demon out of a fortune-telling slave girl. Accused by Philippi's magistrates of throwing the city into confusion, they were beaten with rods and tossed into prison (vv. 19–23). At midnight, God sent an earthquake that rattled loose the prisoners' chains and shook open the cell doors. Also shaken was the jailer, who received the gospel from Paul's outstretched hand and, like Lydia, opened his home to the battered evangelists (vv. 25–34).

In the morning, the magistrates tried to quietly sweep Paul and company out of town, but Paul demanded that the whole affair be made public. They had wrongly beaten a Roman citizen, and he wasn't about to let them off the hook that easily (vv. 35–39). Besides, he needed time for one last meeting with his dear friends.

> And they went out of the prison and entered the house of Lydia, and when they saw the brethren, they encouraged them and departed. (v. 40)

Don't you wish you could have been there? You can almost hear Paul's irrepressible confidence in God as he challenges them to stay the course of faith. Before he leaves, they embrace and pray together, mingling their tears as they commit their lives to each other and to the Lord.

Paul was no paper face on a church missionary bulletin board to these believers. He held a central place in their hearts; and they, a central place in his (see Phil. 1:7). As the church members waved good-bye to Paul, their relationship with him entered a different phase. Without realizing it, the Philippians stepped into a new and vital role in God's missions strategy—they became senders.

Senders and the Sent: The Signs of Caring

Senders and sent have a lot in common. Both are called by God—one to stay, the other to go. Both are missionaries—one fights the battle from the homefront; the other, on the front lines. Within the soul of every sender burns the same flame that ignites the soul of every missionary on the field: the passion to make disciples of all nations. Senders may never leave their own city, but in their hearts, they see the world. And through the hands of those they send, they touch the world too.

The Philippians reached their world by partnering with Paul in his ministry. As we page through the book of Philippians, let's look for the ways they participated with him and the signs that showed they cared.

Grace

We don't have to look far through chapter 1 to find the first sign. Paul writes,

> For it is only right for me to feel this way about you all, because I have you in my heart, since both in my imprisonment and in the defense and confirmation of the gospel, you all are partakers of grace with me. (v. 7)

Their spirits fed on the same grace that nourished Paul. A person who lives by grace allows others to follow God's will freely and doesn't squeeze them in a vice of expectations and guilt. Paul apparently felt that freedom from the Philippians and appreciated their gracious attitude toward him.

Love

In verse 8, he expresses the depths of his feelings:

> For God is my witness, how I long for you all with the affection of Christ Jesus.

The Philippians were family to Paul. They accepted him for who he was; they demonstrated thoughtfulness; they kept in touch with him and showed an interest in his needs. They truly loved him, and he returned their warm affection.

Knowledge

The Philippians communicated their love by keeping current on Paul's situation. The apostle, under house arrest in Rome, fills in some of the details for them in verses 12 and 13:

> Now I want you to know, brethren, that my circumstances have turned out for the greater progress of the gospel, so that my imprisonment in the cause of Christ has become well known throughout the whole praetorian guard and to everyone else.

With this information, they could pray more effectively for Paul—and pray they did!

Prayer

In verse 19, Paul expresses his reliance on their prayers:

> For I know that this shall turn out for my deliverance
> through your prayers and the provision of the Spirit
> of Jesus Christ.

It didn't matter that they were living hundreds of miles away from Paul. Linked by God's satellite system of prayer, they were right there with him, witnessing to the soldiers and helping to free him from Roman custody. That's the power of intercessory prayer.

Sometimes, though, missionaries need a physical touch. The Philippians sensed that need in Paul and sent him a special visitor, Epaphroditus.

Sending an Encourager

Epaphroditus took many risks in coming to Paul, for Rome was an inhospitable place for Christians. In such a large, unfamiliar city he did not know which dark dungeon hid the apostle. As the friend of an imprisoned Christian, whom could he trust? It was a dangerous venture, one which almost cost him his life. After Paul had sent him back to Philippi, he mentions the perils Epaphroditus endured on his behalf:

> But I thought it necessary to send to you Epaphro-
> ditus, my brother and fellow worker and fellow sol-
> dier, who is also your messenger and minister to my
> need; because he was longing for you all and was
> distressed because you had heard that he was sick.
> For indeed he was sick to the point of death, but God
> had mercy on him, and not on him only but also
> on me, lest I should have sorrow upon sorrow. There-
> fore I have sent him all the more eagerly in order
> that when you see him again you may rejoice and I
> may be less concerned about you. Therefore receive
> him in the Lord with all joy, and hold men like him
> in high regard; because he came close to death for
> the work of Christ, risking his life to complete what
> was deficient in your service to me. (2:25–30)

Sending Gifts

The last sign of the Philippians' caring spirit is the gift of money that Epaphroditus brought with him for Paul. This wasn't the first time they had given generously. After he left Macedonia, Paul says, "No church shared with me in the matter of giving and receiving but you alone" (4:15). Paul was thrilled about their gift, not for his own sake—he was content to live with humble means or in prosperity (see vv. 11–12)—but for their sake.

> Not that I seek the gift itself, but I seek for the profit which increases to your account. But I have received everything in full, and have an abundance; I am amply supplied, having received from Epaphroditus what you have sent, a fragrant aroma, an acceptable sacrifice, well-pleasing to God. (vv. 17–18)

What about You?

Are you struggling to clear the hurdle of indifference toward the lost around the world? One way to overcome that obstacle is to realize how important you are to God's program as a "sender." You're needed! Did you know that?

God's enemy often swings us to one of two extremes: he overplays the significance of those who go, or he underplays the value of those who send. The fact is, *both* are necessary and equally valuable to God. As Paul highlighted in his letter to the Romans:

> "Whoever will call upon the name of the Lord will be saved." How then shall they call upon Him in whom they have not believed? And how shall they believe in Him whom they have not heard? And how shall they hear without a preacher? And how shall they preach unless they are sent? Just as it is written, "How beautiful are the feet of those who bring glad tidings of good things!" (Rom. 10:13–15)

Living Insights

Charles Swindoll relates an experience in which a certain "sender" played a crucial role in his life.

> When Cynthia and I first were led by God to change careers and to enter seminary and to begin . . . ministry as our vocational service, which was something

I had resisted for the longest time, we changed our whole life. In fact, we sold our home that we had bought in the outskirts of Houston, Texas, and we moved to Dallas. And we knew, really, no one. . . .

And we set up housekeeping in a little, tiny apartment. It was really a dump. I mean, it was one of those places with hot and cold running rats. You know, those places they finally just condemned. I heard a friend say not long ago, "When we lived there, there wasn't a single roach in the place. They were all married and had a litter of roaches." I mean, there were roaches everywhere. I'm glad to say it's all been torn down. But we didn't know anybody. We didn't have any money. In fact, we had a little indebtedness we had to deal with.

But unknown to us when we came, there was a man in our home church who took an interest in our lives. And he's one of the great heroes of my past. You wouldn't know him if I called his name. He'd be embarrassed if I named him publicly, and so I won't. But year after year after year, he paid our tuition. Not only ours, but twelve or fourteen other fellas who were there from the same church. Regularly. Never once, never once did I have to write him and ask for help. In fact, I wrote him thank-you's and he said, "Would you not take your time to write thank-you's?" He said, "I want to thank *you* for giving me this opportunity for service."[2]

Are you excited about being a sender? Then let the following questions help turn your eagerness into action.

Whom could you help send? Write down this person's name.

Ask yourself these questions:
How can I demonstrate grace toward this person?

---

2. From the sermon "Clearing the Hurdle of Indifference," previously titled "Senders Care," given at the Evangelical Free Church of Fullerton, California, February 8, 1987.

How can I show love to this person?

How can I stay informed?

How can I make sure to pray for him or her regularly?

How can I encourage him or her?

What can I give to help this person in their ministry the most? Money? Material things? Some other resource?

Think of how effective that man from Houston was as he furthered God's kingdom by helping send Chuck Swindoll and those other young seminarians into the ministry. You can be a sender too. The world awaits!

Chapter 8

CLEARING THE HURDLE
OF SELFISHNESS

Selections from Philippians

In the late 1700s, when the United States was still an infant nation, William Carey was rearing a newborn movement of his own. Considered the father of modern missions, Carey spent forty years in India proclaiming Christ to the Hindus and pioneering many of the methods that missionaries use today.

None of Carey's great accomplishments, however, would have been possible without the help of the dedicated Christians who stayed home—the senders. One supporter, Andrew Fuller, recalled Carey's request for help when he volunteered for the mission to India:

> "We saw that there was a gold mine in India, but it was as deep as the center of the earth. I asked, 'Who will venture to explore it?' Carey replied, 'I will venture to go down, but remember that you' meaning Sutcliff, Ryland, and myself, 'must hold the ropes.'"[1]

Through the years, these men kept their commitment, firmly holding the lifeline that sustained Carey and his family through the many shivering nights of loneliness and scorching days of defeat. The example of these faithful senders challenges us to consider how well we're holding the rope for our self-sacrificing missionaries on the field. We can't expect them to bear alone the load of fulfilling Christ's command,

> "Go into all the world and preach the gospel to all creation." (Mark 16:15)

All of us must be willing to make sacrifices in reaching the lost, which means we first need to overcome the barrier of selfishness.

Senders in the Bible

From the very beginning, unselfish "senders" have played a vital

1. Basil Miller, *William Carey: The Father of Modern Missions* (Minneapolis, Minn.: Bethany House Publishers, 1980), pp. 41–42.

role in God's plan of redemption. Take a look at a familiar verse that you may never have seen this way before:

> "For God so loved the world, that He gave His only begotten Son, that whoever believes in Him should not perish, but have eternal life." (John 3:16)

God the Father could have come to earth Himself, but He sent His only Son instead. He was the first sender; and Jesus, the first one sent. Missions is simply an imitation of their example.

The church in Antioch followed God's pattern of love when it sent its best teachers, Barnabas and Saul, to the foreign field.

> Now there were at Antioch, in the church that was there, prophets and teachers: Barnabas, and Simeon who was called Niger, and Lucius of Cyrene, and Manaen who had been brought up with Herod the tetrarch, and Saul. And while they were ministering to the Lord and fasting, the Holy Spirit said, "Set apart for Me Barnabas and Saul for the work to which I have called them." Then, when they had fasted and prayed and laid their hands on them, they sent them away. (Acts 13:1–3)

Like soldiers going off to war, Saul and Barnabas marched to the front lines to battle Satan's forces. Today, our missionaries are still fighting the same war. How can we best support them? The same way we support our GI sons and daughters during wartime. We pray for them, send news and photos from home, let them know we're thinking of them, ship them care packages . . . whatever we can think of to lift their spirits and remind them that we're still holding the rope.

Senders in Action

In the previous chapter, we highlighted the Philippians as model senders. Let's return to their example for seven specific ways we can clear the hurdle of selfishness and get involved in the lives of our missionary troops on the field.

Consistent Participation

In Philippians 1:5, we see that Paul thanked God for the Philippians because of their "participation in the gospel from the first day until now." From the time they met Paul, they locked arms with him and the gospel message he taught. And when he left Philippi, he wasn't "out of sight, out of mind" to them. They stuck by him consistently.

How consistently do we support our missionaries? Does our interest glow like the full moon during missions week at church, then wane to a sliver in the weeks that follow?

Small but regular encouragement goes much further than one enthusiastic contribution followed by nothing. The most loving gestures in any relationship are those made faithfully over time.

Abundant Love

The Philippians certainly had a loving relationship with Paul. Feel his love for them in the following verses:

> For it is only right for me to feel this way about you all, because I have you in my heart, since both in my imprisonment and in the defense and confirmation of the gospel, you all are partakers of grace with me. For God is my witness, how I long for you all with the affection of Christ Jesus. And this I pray, that your love may abound still more and more in real knowledge and all discernment. (1:7–9)

Living in another culture where the people speak a different language, eat different food, and enjoy different customs can make anyone feel very alone. For missionaries, familiar words from home—a letter, a videotape, or a phone call—can soothe the emotions like a cool cloth on a fevered brow.

Prayer Support

Prayer is often the best expression of love. For Paul, the Philippians' prayers gave him an anchor of hope during the storm of his imprisonment in Rome. Their prayers and Christ's Spirit filled him with indomitable confidence:

> For I know that this shall turn out for my deliverance through your prayers and the provision of the Spirit of Jesus Christ. (v. 19)

How can we make our prayer time for our missionaries more meaningful?

- *Be informed.* Collect information about the missionaries, their work, and the people they're trying to reach.

- *Be specific.* Avoid the God-bless-the-missionaries type of prayer. Pray for the marital, emotional, financial, or ministry needs each family may have.

- *Be bold.* Ask God for giant steps forward rather than praying merely for survival. As William Carey once wrote: "Expect great things from God; attempt great things for God."[2]

- *Be practical.* What would you like people to pray for if you were in the field? Pray for those practical things.

- *Be faithful.* Pray every day, just like you would if the missionary was your son or daughter, brother or sister.

Unity and Solidarity

Missionaries need to know that their supporting churches are stable, unified, and strong. As Paul wrote to the home church in Philippi:

> Only conduct yourselves in a manner worthy of the gospel of Christ; so that whether I come and see you or remain absent, I may hear of you that you are standing firm in one spirit, with one mind striving together for the faith of the gospel. (v. 27)

When a church splits or is battered by scandal, the far-away missionaries feel the blows too. Membership drops, donations dry up, and the missionaries are left on their own in a foreign land without a foundation to rest on. Peace of mind comes with knowing that their home church is secure.

Shared Joy

The bond Paul had with the Philippians went far below the surface to the place of inner joy—the place where true friendship is found. In the following verses, Paul opened his heart to his readers.

But even if I am being poured out as a drink offering

---

2. William Carey, as quoted by Ruth Tucker in "William Carey: Father of Modern Missions," *Great Leaders of the Christian Church*, ed. John D. Woodbridge (Chicago, Ill.: Moody Press, 1988), p. 309.

upon the sacrifice and service of your faith, I rejoice and share my joy with you all. And you too, I urge you, rejoice in the same way and share your joy with me. (2:17–18)

One of the ways we can share our joy in living is through humor. Commentator Helmut Thielecke once wrote about the importance of laughter in the life of faith:

> Should we not see that lines of laughter about the eyes are just as much marks of faith as are the lines of care and seriousness? Is it only earnestness that is baptized? Is laughter pagan? We have already allowed too much that is good to be lost to the church and cast many pearls before swine. A church is in a bad way when it banishes laughter from the sanctuary and leaves it to the cabaret, the nightclub and the toastmasters.[3]

Is your missionary correspondence too serious? Liven it up with a creative flare. Send a funny article or cartoon from the newspaper. Share the antics and discoveries of your four-year-old. As the old Swedish proverb says, "A sorrow shared is halved; a joy shared is doubled." The lighter side of life may be just what your missionaries need to buoy their spirits.

Positive Attitude

A positive attitude is one of the best gifts we can give our missionaries. Notice the positive attitude Paul expressed in these verses:

> Brethren, I do not regard myself as having laid hold of it yet; but one thing I do: forgetting what lies behind and reaching forward to what lies ahead, I press on toward the goal for the prize of the upward call of God in Christ Jesus. Let us therefore, as many as are perfect, have this attitude; and if in anything you have a different attitude, God will reveal that also to you. (3:13–15)

What are the goals we press on toward? What are our dreams?

---

3. Helmut Thielecke, as quoted by J. Oswald Sanders, in *Spiritual Leadership*, rev. ed. (Chicago, Ill.: Moody Press, 1980), p. 84.

What is God showing us about our future? By sharing our vision and excitement about what lies ahead, we encourage our missionaries to get excited about God's possibilities for themselves.

Personal and Financial Resources

The last treasure to share is our resources: money, skills, time. Paul affirmed the Philippians for their gracious generosity:

> But I rejoiced in the Lord greatly, that now at last you have revived your concern for me; indeed, you were concerned before, but you lacked opportunity. . . . Nevertheless, you have done well to share with me in my affliction. And you yourselves also know, Philippians, that at the first preaching of the gospel, after I departed from Macedonia, no church shared with me in the matter of giving and receiving but you alone; for even in Thessalonica you sent a gift more than once for my needs. (4:10, 14–16)

Because of the Philippians' thoughtful care, Paul could say with gratitude, "I am amply supplied" (v. 18).

Can our missionaries say the same thing?

Senders Today

All around the world are spiritual gold mines—deep caverns in which converts for Christ wait like treasures to be unearthed. Who are the William Careys of our generation, willing to go down and do the digging? Who are the Sutcliffes, Rylands, and Fullers willing to hold the ropes?

If we buy into the world's philosophy, which says, "You only go around once, so you better grab all the pleasure you can," then we'll never be willing to step out of our comfort zones and serve the Lord. But if we can clear that hurdle of selfishness and put Christ first in our lives, no sacrifice is too great. No obstacle is too high in obeying God's call.

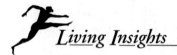

Living Insights

Clearing the hurdle of selfishness is the first and biggest step in reaching others for Christ. The next step is to make some practical changes in our lives, specifically concerning our involvement in missions.

In the following self-evaluation, circle the letter of the response that best completes each statement for you. This will help you measure how well you're doing as a sender.

Self-Evaluation Profile for Senders[4]

- *When it comes to the biblical understanding of missions, I . . .*
  a. can explain how every book of the Bible relates to world evangelization.
  b. am able to show how missions is the backbone of the Bible.
  c. understand the strategy of missions in the Old Testament.
  d. can quote two verses that emphasize world evangelism.
  e. can name one verse that relates to missions.

- *When it comes to missions education, I . . .*
  a. assist others in understanding what God is doing in missions.
  b. am taking a missions class.
  c. read several missions books a year.
  d. dialogue with missionaries.
  e. read missionary prayer letters.
  f. read with interest the information about missions in the church bulletin.
  g. have no desire to learn what God is doing around the globe.
  h. conscientiously avoid any missions information.

- *When it comes to prayer, I . . .*
  a. regularly fast and pray for specific requests from missionaries.
  b. write to missionaries asking for specific prayer requests and then pray for them.
  c. pray that family and friends may become missionaries.
  d. pray weekly for specific missionaries.
  e. pray occasionally for missionaries.
  f. pray with the pastor on Sunday mornings for a missionary.

4. Adapted from a chart in "A Quick Measure for the Missions Sender," distributed by the First Evangelical Free Church of Fullerton, California.

- *When it comes to my church's missions emphasis, I . . .*
  a. assist others in knowing what our church is doing in missions.
  b. volunteer to help our visiting missionaries with housing, transportation, etc.
  c. eagerly look forward to our missions conference.
  d. personally know four or five of our church's missionaries.
  e. can name three of our church's missionaries.
  f. am content that missions is happening in our church but am not personally concerned about missions.

- *When it comes to encouraging missionaries, I . . .*
  a. visit them at their assignments.
  b. send care packages two or three times a year.
  c. call missionaries on their birthdays.
  d. write letters to missionaries.
  e. seek out opportunities to meet missionaries.
  f. talk to a missionary when introduced to one.
  g. don't do anything with missionaries.

- *When it comes to giving, I . . .*
  a. encourage others to give to a particular missionary.
  b. sacrifice to give to missions.
  c. look for creative ways to save/earn money to give to missions.
  d. support church missionaries outside of giving to the general fund.
  e. give $10 a month to a missionary.
  f. give minimally to the church.

- *When it comes to missionary recruitment, I . . .*
  a. ask God if He wants my children to become missionaries.
  b. ask God if I should become a missionary.
  c. assist potential missionaries who are studying by offering low-cost housing and/or financial assistance.
  d. encourage others to consider missions as a vocation.
  e. actively educate others on the need for more missionaries around the world.
  f. pray that God would raise up missionaries from our church.

Your answers in the *a* and *b* levels show that you're doing great! If you're in the *c* and *d* levels, you are coming along. Levels *e* and *f* put you on the threshold of being a sender. And any *g* and *h* answers reveal a need to get serious about missions.

How do you measure up? What do you need to do to move up

to the next level? By making solid plans and carrying them through, you'll be well on your way to becoming a world-class sender!

Plan of Action

_____

_____

_____

_____

_____

_____

_____

_____

_____

_____

_____

_____

_____

_____

_____

_____

_____

_____

_____

_____

_____

_____

_____

Chapter 9

CLEARING THE HURDLE OF CARNALITY

Selections from 1 Corinthians

Prone to wander, Lord, I feel it,
Prone to leave the God I love.[1]

When Robert Robinson penned this line, he seemed to peer across the centuries into our souls. His confession is our confession. Like him, we love the Lord and long to please Him; but how easily the desire to please ourselves turns our heads and pulls us away from God's warm embrace.

The apostle Paul felt that same pull within his heart. The result was a fierce inner battle:

> For we know that the Law is spiritual; but I am of flesh, sold into bondage to sin. For that which I am doing, I do not understand; for I am not practicing what I would like to do, but I am doing the very thing I hate. . . . For I know that nothing good dwells in me, that is, in my flesh; for the wishing is present in me, but the doing of the good is not. For the good that I wish, I do not do; but I practice the very evil that I do not wish. . . . For I joyfully concur with the law of God in the inner man, but I see a different law in the members of my body, waging war against the law of my mind, and making me a prisoner of the law of sin which is in my members. Wretched man that I am! (Rom. 7:14–15, 18–19, 22–24a)

What is it that inclines us to do the opposite of what we know is best? When we truly love the Lord, why do we wander from Him? Just as Dr. Jekyll struggled against his Mr. Hyde, so we are torn by a force lurking inside each of us: the flesh. To clear this hurdle in our lives, let's take a closer look at the flesh and what theologians call "the warfare of the soul."

---

1. Robert Robinson, "Come Thou Fount of Every Blessing," in *The Hymnal for Worship and Celebration* (Waco, Tex.: Word Music, 1986), no. 2.

The Struggle against the Flesh

What Paul conveys from his own experience in Romans 7, he teaches in Galatians 5:17. In the Living Bible, the verse reads,

> For we naturally love to do evil things that are just the opposite from the things that the Holy Spirit tells us to do; and the good things we want to do when the Spirit has his way with us are just the opposite of our natural desires. These two forces within us are constantly fighting each other to win control over us, and our wishes are never free from their pressures.

Did you notice the phrases "constantly fighting" and "never free"? From our spiritual birth to our physical death, the Holy Spirit wars against our flesh—that powerful inner force that pursues its own ends apart from God.

The flesh can never be reformed. Our sin nature remains just as stubborn, selfish, and arrogant as it was before we were saved. We may mature spiritually and assume respected positions of leadership in the church, but our flesh never grows up. In fact, the more we mature, the greater the inner conflict. Wickedness is always raving inside us, ready to raise its fist and take control.

Three Types of People

The degree to which the flesh or the Spirit controls us determines where we stand spiritually. In 1 Corinthians, Paul identifies three types of people based on that measure.

The Natural Person

The unsaved person who is completely controlled by the flesh is called the "natural man."[2] This person "does not accept the things of the Spirit of God" (1 Cor. 2:14a)—their heart's welcome mat is pulled in and the door bolted against spiritual truths. Also, the things of

---

2. Natural people still struggle morally, but "this is not a spiritual struggle. It is a rational struggle, a conflict between the human reason and conscience, on the one hand, and his will and desire on the other. . . . The battle is not waged against all sins, but only against some of them, and for the most part only against certain external and outwardly offensive sins. The struggle is not waged against sin as sin." Herman Bavinck in *Reasonable Faith*, as quoted by Anthony A. Hoekema, "The Struggle between Old and New Natures in the Converted Man," from the *Bulletin of the Evangelical Theological Society*, Spring 1962, p. 48.

God "are foolishness to him, and he cannot understand them, because they are spiritually appraised" (v. 14b). Just as whales' songs out of the ocean depths remain a mystery to us, so the deep realities of life in God remain incomprehensible to the natural person.

The Spiritual Person

In contrast, the spiritual person is controlled by the Holy Spirit. Consequently,

> he who is spiritual appraises all things, yet he himself is appraised by no man. For who has known the mind of the Lord, that he should instruct Him? But we have the mind of Christ. (vv. 15–16)

With the mind of Christ, we are able to hear the Spirit's words through a new mental process. As a result, subjects like sin, grace, and forgiveness are no longer unintelligible but bursting with meaning and power. The Spirit of Christ becomes our teacher, encourager, and guide. Yielding to His direction, we are able to glorify God with deeds of holiness—something that was impossible in our natural state no matter how "moral" we thought we were.

Unfortunately, the flesh does not pack up and move away when the Spirit moves in. It glares at the Intruder, who has invaded its domain, and determines to claw its way back into control.

The Carnal Person

Within the Christian, the battle between the flesh and the Spirit is fierce, but in the end, we're the ones who determine the outcome. If we give in to the flesh and quench the Spirit's power, we enter a state of carnality. The word *carnal* comes from a Latin word that simply means "flesh." We become "fleshly" (1 Cor. 3:3).

From the church's beginnings, Christians have struggled to clear the high hurdle of carnality. Weighed down by the flesh, believers have stumbled into destructive patterns of sin—the likes of which Paul describes in Galatians 5:

> immorality, impurity, sensuality, idolatry, sorcery, enmities, strife, jealousy, outbursts of anger, disputes, dissensions, factions, envying, drunkenness, carousing, and things like these. (vv. 19–21a)

No fruit of the Spirit sprouts from the branches of the carnal person's life (compare vv. 22–23). No love, no joy, no peace. Only the shriveled remains of a once-vibrant faith.

For the rest of this chapter, let's focus on this state of carnality. What do we know about it? How can we spot it in ourselves? Most importantly, what are some ways to overcome it?

Characteristics of Carnality

The Corinthian church is the most notorious for its struggles with the flesh. From Paul's rebuke in 1 Corinthians 3, we discover four characteristics of carnality.

The Carnal Person Is a Believer

He begins verse 1, "And I, *brethren*. . . ." Earlier in his letter, he addresses his readers as "those who have been sanctified in Christ Jesus" and "saints by calling" (1:2). He acknowledges that they have been "enriched in Him" and "are not lacking in any gift" (vv. 5, 7). Paul also assures them of their salvation, saying that Christ "shall also confirm you to the end, blameless in the day of our Lord Jesus Christ" (v. 8). And in verse 10, he writes, "I exhort you, *brethren*"— the same word he uses in chapter 3.

It's clear that, despite their carnality, the Corinthians were still Christians. God didn't disown these prodigal sons and daughters because they wandered away from Him, and neither will He disown us.

The Carnal Person Lacks Spiritual Growth

Once we become a child of God, we stay a child of God. But God doesn't want us to remain little children; He wants us to grow up. The Corinthians, unfortunately, were still clinging to their baby bottles.

> And I, brethren, could not speak to you as to spiritual men, but as to men of flesh, as to babes in Christ. I gave you milk to drink, not solid food; for you were not yet able to receive it. Indeed, even now you are not yet able. (3:1–2)

We can bear with babies' dependency and demands, impulsiveness and irritability because we know they're not yet capable of getting their needs met any other way. However, adults who continue to act like babies—showing no manners, no self-control, and no real concern for others—strain the limits of our tolerance. Why? Because they are now capable of, and therefore responsible for, greater maturity in their behavior.

Paul yearned to impart solid truth to the Corinthians and relate with them as fellow adults. But they had latched on to their babyhood with a white-knuckled grip, and their prolonged infancy rendered them mere "men of flesh."

Carnal Christians, like Peter Pan, don't want to grow up. They want to be fed a diet of sweet, easy-to-swallow platitudes. They like being entertained; and when they don't get their way, they stamp their feet and raise a fuss until someone gives in. The most difficult people in the church are often those who have grown old in the Lord—but have not grown up.

The Carnal Person Focuses on the Horizontal

Another characteristic of carnal Christians is that their horizontal connections with other people take precedence over their vertical relationship with God. Like children on the playground choosing sides for kickball, they often divide themselves into cliques and bicker over who's better than who. Paul sees this happening in the Corinthian church and confronts them:

> For you are still fleshly. For since there is jealousy
> and strife among you, are you not fleshly, and are
> you not walking like mere men? For when one says,
> "I am of Paul," and another, "I am of Apollos," are
> you not mere men? (vv. 3–4)

Carnal Christians acclaim their favorite leader and disclaim the rest. Soon factions develop. Then divisions. Then church splits. And who's watching the debacle? The unsaved, who most need to know that Christ really does make a difference.

Carnal People Resemble Non-Christians

Exasperated, Paul asks the Corinthians: "Are you not fleshly,[3] and are you not walking like mere men?" (v. 3). The answer is yes. They were behaving according to the standards of ordinary, selfish, natural people. Their flesh was in control—which made them capable of looking, acting, and talking just like the unsaved.

---

3. In verse 1, he called them "men of *flesh*"—in Greek, the word is *sarkinos* and means "made of flesh." But here in verse 3 he uses the word *fleshly*—in Greek, *sarkikos*, which means "controlled by the flesh." Fritz Rienecker, *A Linguistic Key to the Greek New Testament*, ed. Cleon L. Rogers, Jr. (Grand Rapids, Mich.: Zondervan Publishing House, Regency Reference Library, 1980), p. 393.

How Carnality Expresses Itself

In the rest of Paul's letter to the Corinthians, he holds up a mirror to reveal several ways they resembled those without Christ.

Activities

The first way concerns their shameful activities. Chapter 5 begins with the shocking revelation that one of the Corinthian believers was living with his stepmother in an incestuous relationship.

> It is actually reported that there is immorality among you, and immorality of such a kind as does not exist even among the Gentiles, that someone has his father's wife. (5:1)

It seems hard to believe that a Christian could do such a thing. Well, we had better believe it. When the flesh dominates a person's life, nothing is taboo.

Attitudes

Concerning the man who was living in sin, Paul admonished the church,

> And you have become arrogant, and have not mourned instead, in order that the one who had done this deed might be removed from your midst. (v. 2)

Instead of falling on their faces before God in humble repentance, the people put their thumbs in their suspenders and crowed, "Look how accepting we are of this sinning brother." In verse 6, Paul tells them that their "boasting is not good." In their attitude of arrogance over their supposed grace, they were really turning an indifferent ear to God's holy standard.

Paul shouts, "Clean out the old leaven" (v. 7)! Get rid of the attitudes of "malice and wickedness" and replace them with "sincerity and truth" (v. 8).

Associations

Third, the people with whom we associate also reveal our carnality. What type of person did Paul warn the Corinthians about? Not the fleshly non-Christians, as we might think, but the fleshly Christians.

> I wrote you in my letter not to associate with immoral people; I did not at all mean with the immoral

people of this world, or with the covetous and swindlers, or with idolaters; for then you would have to go out of the world. But actually, I wrote to you not to associate with any so-called brother if he should be an immoral person, or covetous, or an idolater, or a reviler, or a drunkard, or a swindler—not even to eat with such a one. (5:9–11)

Our friends help shape our character, whether we realize it or not. We can't run with an angry person without becoming angry ourselves. We can't run with a sensual person without becoming sensual ourselves. "Bad company corrupts good morals" (15:33).

Appetites

Finally, carnality expresses itself in our appetites. Paul describes the ancient Hebrews exiting Egypt as examples that "we should not crave evil things, as they also craved" (10:6). Though the word *crave* can mean a morally neutral longing, "it usually denotes evil desire," with "disobedience, not irrationality," at the root.[4] The quest to sate these ravenous desires can lead to idolatry (v. 7), immorality (v. 8), presumption (v. 9), and resentful grumbling (v. 10).

The Corinthians, tragically, did not learn from history very well. They celebrated the Lord's Supper with a raucous banquet, where church members scrambled for their own dinners if they wanted anything to eat. Some went away hungry. Some even got drunk (see 11:20–22). No one worshiped the Lord. What a shameful scene!

"For this reason," Paul told them, "many among you are weak and sick, and a number sleep" (v. 30). In other words, some had died because of their carnality. That's tough discipline.

Conclusion

What do we do with a lesson like this? Our first response is usually to hold it up like a yardstick against other people's lives. "Let's see, how does my spouse measure up? Hmm, needs a little work. I thought so."

Paul advises the Corinthians and us today, "Let a man examine himself" (v. 28). For "if we judged ourselves rightly, we should not

---

4. Gerhard Kittel and Gerhard Friedrich, eds., *Theological Dictionary of the New Testament*, translated and abridged by Geoffrey W. Bromiley (1985; reprint, Grand Rapids, Mich.: William B. Eerdmans Publishing Co., 1992), p. 340.

be judged" (v. 31).

The first place to look for signs of carnality is in our own mirrors. Are we growing spiritually? Are we focusing on people rather than God? Do we see the fleshly actions, attitudes, associations, and appetites of a non-Christian in our life?

Self-examination is never easy. But if it results in repentance and confession, God assures us that He will bring cleansing and restoration. On the other hand, if we rationalize our sin, dig our heels in to defend our fleshly habits, and resist change, we open ourselves to God's discipline.

As much as we'd like to, we can't get rid of our flesh. But the good news is, we *can* put the Spirit in control. Only He can give us the strength to clear the hurdle of carnality.

Living Insights

The ancient Greeks offered a pearl of good advice: "Know thyself." Identify your strengths; admit your weaknesses. Recognize the signs of greed's invasion, of envy's assault, of pride's subtle schemes. Stay alert to the ways of the flesh. Know your limits.

That's easy to say but hard to do. Because the moment we think we've cornered our fleshly nature, it broadsides us with a selfish attitude or a spiteful spirit. The ancient Hebrews had another saying,

> "The heart is more deceitful than all else
> And is desperately sick;
> Who can understand it?" (Jer. 17:9)

That's why we need the Holy Spirit's light to expose our flesh's destructive ways. David prayed,

> Search me, O God, and know my heart;
> Try me and know my anxious thoughts;
> And see if there be any hurtful way in me,
> And lead me in the everlasting way. (Ps. 139:23–24)

In this Living Insight, we'd like you to set aside some time for reflection. Invite the Holy Spirit to hold a mirror to your soul so you can take a hard look at your sin nature. Examine your activities, attitudes, associations, and appetites, and write down the fleshly tendencies you see.

Mirror to My Soul

Turning these areas over to the Spirit's control, ask the Lord to lead you in "the everlasting way." Record what you need to do this week to follow Him instead of the flesh.

God's Everlasting Way for Me

Chapter 10

CLEARING THE HURDLE
OF CONFUSION
Selected Scriptures

In their book *God's Will: You Can Know It*, Leslie and Bernice Flynn illustrate some popular ways of discerning God's will.

> A lady received a brochure outlining a tour to Israel. She had the time, money, and strength to take the trip but wondered if it were God's will. Rereading the pamphlet just before retiring, she noted that the airplane for the trip was a 747 jet. She tossed all night, restlessly arguing the pros and cons of fulfilling a lifelong ambition to visit the Holy Land. Awaking in the morning, she looked at her digital clock. It said 7:47. She exclaimed, "It must be the Lord's will for me to take that tour." . . .
>
> A pastor who had served as a deacon in his preordination days, toyed with the idea of buying an honorary doctor of divinity from a diploma mill. Reading 1 Timothy 3:13, he was confident he had his answer, "For they that have used the office of a deacon well purchase to themselves a good degree."[1]

These methods may strike us as unbelievable, but who of us can honestly say we've never done anything like that? Because we yearn for God to guide us, we're willing to read almost anything as a sign from heaven—especially if it confirms what we really want to do.

The hocus-pocus method of knowing God's will can backfire, though. Like the young man who needed a car but didn't know which one to buy. He saw the color yellow in his dreams one night, so the next morning he went looking for a yellow car. He got one alright—a lemon!

"Do not be foolish," Paul writes, "but understand what the will of the Lord is" (Eph. 5:17). God commands us to know His will, but sometimes trying to figure it out can be downright confusing.

---

1. Leslie and Bernice Flynn, *God's Will: You Can Know It* (Wheaton, Ill.: Scripture Press Publications, Victor Books, 1979), pp. 9–10.

How can the high school senior know which college God wants him or her to attend? Which vocation to pursue? Whom to marry? And how many children to have?

How can people know which church to join? How can the employee know whether to accept the out-of-state transfer? How can the older couple know when it's time to retire?

How can *any* of us discern God's will?

Two Categories of God's Will

Through the centuries, many a scholar has pulled his beard out trying to comprehend the vast universe we call God's will. Gazing into the theological sky, we see two galaxies of His will that seemingly collide—His sovereignty and our freedom. In some inscrutable way, however, they coexist in perfect balance.

God's Determined Will

On the one hand, God has already sovereignly determined what will happen in our lives. As the supreme ruler of heaven and earth, "He chose us in Him before the foundation of the world . . . predestined us to adoption as sons through Jesus Christ . . . works all things after the counsel of His will" (Eph. 1:4a, 5a, 11b). He alone steers the ship.

Boastful King Nebuchadnezzar learned this truth the hard way. God reduced him to the level of an animal until he recognized who was the true captain of the universe. When his reason returned, he proclaimed,

> "And all the inhabitants of the earth are accounted
>   as nothing,
> But He does according to His will in the host of
>   heaven
> And among the inhabitants of earth;
> And no one can ward off His hand
> Or say to Him, 'What hast Thou done?'"
> (Dan. 4:35)

In his book *Knowing God's Will and Doing It!*, J. Grant Howard, Jr., describes God's determined will in these impressive terms:

> It is inevitable, unconditional, immutable, irresistible, comprehensive, and purposeful. It is also, for

the most part, unpredictable.[2]

The fact is, we don't know what His determined will is until after it happens. It's as if God has scripted and filmed the story of our lives, He knows ahead of time what the next scene holds. But we don't. We're viewing the film for the first time. However, we do know how the story ends. If we've trusted Christ for our salvation, we look forward to a happily-ever-after ending in heaven. That's the only aspect of God's determined will we can know for certain.[3]

God's Desired Will

Although we don't know what the next scene of our life holds, we can know what God *wants* it to hold. Howard writes:

> The determined will is that which will happen. The desired will is that which he *wants to happen* in every person's life. It is not inevitable. It may or may not happen. It is not unconditional. It is based on our decisions. It is not irresistible. We can choose not to do it. And most significant, it is not a mystery. It is something we can know and should do.[4]

Wait a minute, God could desire something and not have it fulfilled? Yes. Take a look at Matthew 23:37.

> "O Jerusalem, Jerusalem, who kills the prophets and stones those who are sent to her! *How often I wanted to gather your children together,* the way a hen gathers her chicks under her wings, and *you were unwilling.*" (emphasis added)

With that same divine passion, God yearns for us to be wise and clearheaded (Eph. 5:15–18), for husbands to love their wives (vv. 25–28), for His people to speak the truth (4:15, 25), for us to steer clear of sexual immorality (5:3). But in His sovereignty, He has given us the freedom to choose our response.

---

2. J. Grant Howard, Jr., *Knowing God's Will—and Doing It!* (Grand Rapids, Mich.: Zondervan Publishing House, 1976), p. 12.

3. Was sin in God's sovereign plan? Yes, and so was His provision for sin, Jesus Christ (Luke 22:22; Acts 2:22–24, 36; 1 Pet. 1:18–21). Does that make God responsible for sin? No, Adam and Eve were responsible for their disobedience, and so are we (see Rom. 3:9–26; James 1:13–18).

4. Howard, *Knowing God's Will*, p. 16.

A simple chart will help clarify the differences between God's determined and desired wills.

Determined Will	Desired Will
• Predestined	• Calls for our cooperation
• Comprehensive, eternal	• Limited, temporal
• It will occur	• It may or may not occur
• Cannot be frustrated	• Can be resisted
• Emphasis: God's sovereignty	• Emphasis: Our responsibility
• Purpose: To glorify God	• Purpose: To glorify God

Two Questions That Need to Be Answered

In light of our responsibility, two questions emerge: How does God make His will known? and, How can I know that I'm in His will? Delving into these issues requires four conditions. First, physical and emotional health, the lack of which fogs our ability to interpret God's will. Second, a true desire to know His will. Third, a willingness to change if needed. And last, faith in Christ, because spiritual sensitivity and discernment are "family truths" that can only be applied by the members of God's family.

With that said, let's dig into the first question.

How Does God Make His Will Known?

God has given us three lights to guide us down the path of His desired will. First, we look to the light of God's Word. Second, we see how our conscience is reading our circumstances. Third, we seek wise counsel from others. To put it succinctly, when we want to know God's will, we need to look up, look in, and look out.

1. *Look up into His face by opening His Word.* God's Word is the brightest beacon showing the way, as the psalmist wrote: "Thy word is a lamp to my feet, And a light to my path" (Ps. 119:105). In it He gives us precepts and principles, specific instructions and general directions. Howard explains,

> The sign that reads "SPEED LIMIT 25 MPH" is a precept. The sign that reads "DRIVE CAREFULLY" is a principle.[5]

5. Howard, *Knowing God's Will*, p. 28.

Precepts are black-and-white, with no grays in between. They are finely tuned commands that remove all guesswork. For example, "Do not associate with a gossip" (Prov. 20:19b); "Do not lie to one another" (Col. 3:9a); "This is the will of God . . . that you abstain from sexual immorality" (1 Thess. 4:3).

Principles, on the other hand, are like umbrellas, covering a variety of situations. For instance, Paul says,

> All things are lawful for me, but not all things are profitable. All things are lawful for me, but I will not be mastered by anything. (1 Cor. 6:12)

Can you identify a principle from that verse? To what specific situations can you apply that principle? The answers require sound interpretation and mature thinking.

In most situations, biblical precepts and principles will illumine the direction God wants us to take. Sometimes, though, each of our choices falls within clear scriptural boundaries. Then what do we do?

2. *Look within to what God is saying through your conscience.* Paul wrote in Philippians 2:

> So then, my beloved, just as you have always obeyed, not as in my presence only, but now much more in my absence, work out your salvation with fear and trembling; for it is God who is at work in you, both to will and to work for His good pleasure. (vv. 12–13)

What does Paul mean in the phrase "work out your salvation"? Simply this: If we have trusted Christ for our salvation, then we have entered a lifestyle called Christianity. Now we must flesh out that lifestyle, experience it, live it out. And we do this in a spirit of "fear and trembling," which essentially means a sensitive heart. This sensitivity produces a deep desire *not* to miss God's direction; so we stay keenly alert to His working, paying close attention to doors He opens and closes.

And yes, closed doors, as Chuck Swindoll points out in his booklet *God's Will,*

> are just as much God's leading as open ones. The believer who wants to do God's will *must* remain sensitive and cooperative, not forcing his way into areas that God closes off. The Lord uses circumstances

and expects us to "read" them with a sensitive, alert conscience.[6]

Sensitive, as you've probably guessed, is the key word here. The Lord promises to guide us:

> "I will instruct you and teach you in the way which
>   you should go;
> I will counsel you with My eye upon you." (Ps. 32:8)

But He warns us not to be uncooperative and stubborn,

> ". . . as the horse or as the mule which have no
>   understanding,
> Whose trappings include bit and bridle to hold them
>   in check." (v. 9a)

Instead, when we feel the Master's hand and hear His voice in the circumstances of life, we should follow Him.

3. *Look outside and listen to the wise counsel of qualified, godly people.* Just as a quarterback calls a time-out to consult the coach about the next play, we need to seek the insight of objective, experienced people—particularly in those fourth-and-one situations when you don't know whether to punt or plow ahead.

The proverb says,

> "Without consultation, plans are frustrated,
> But with many counselors they succeed."
> (Prov. 15:22)

We can see this truth in action in Moses' life, when Jethro, his father-in-law, advised him about how to better manage the crowds coming to him (Exod. 18:13–27). Also, the apostle Paul exhorted older women in the early church to counsel the younger women about marriage and good character (Titus 2:3–5). Today, those in business regularly hire consultants to help them succeed. Schools do too. Seeking counsel, then, is simply a smart thing to do.

How Can I Know I'm in God's Will?

After we've made our decision, how do we know we've chosen

---

6. Charles R. Swindoll, *God's Will: Biblical Direction for Living* (Portland, Oreg.: Multnomah Press, 1981), p. 17. For an example of this kind of sensitivity to closed doors, look at Paul's experience in Acts 16:6–10.

God's way? First, whether things work out happily or trouble inten-
sifies, we have inner peace. Paul says, "Let the peace of Christ rule
in your hearts" (Col. 3:15a). His settled assurance in our hearts is
our most important barometer, letting us know if we've made the
right choice.

Also, when you're in God's will, you experience a sense of
satisfaction like nothing else could offer. No other job would be as
fulfilling—even one that paid a higher salary. No other place to
live would feel like home. You know you're right where you belong.

Finally, and perhaps most importantly, you'll know your choices
are in God's will when they glorify Him—when they reflect His
holiness, His righteousness, His purity, His kindness, His truth, His
love, His life. As Jesus told us,

> "Let your light shine before men in such a way that
> they may see your good works, and glorify your Fa-
> ther who is in heaven." (Matt. 5:16)

There's no higher measure than this.

Living Insights
STUDY ONE

Are you trying to discover God's will in a specific area of your
life? Take a moment to jot down the nature of the decision
confronting you.

_____

_____

_____

_____

Have you turned to the three lights mentioned in the chapter
to illumine your path? For example, what guidance is God's Word
giving you?

_____

_____

_____

_____

What direction do you sense from your circumstances and con-science?

_____

_____

_____

_____

What advice have qualified counselors offered?

_____

_____

_____

_____

What direction seems to bring the most peace, satisfaction, and glory to God?

_____

_____

_____

_____

Living Insights   STUDY TWO

Before you jog off the track and head for a tall, cool glass of Gatorade, spend some time looking back at the hurdles we've encountered. Which truths about overcoming each obstacle have impacted and encouraged you the most?

Unpreparedness (not being ready for Christ's return)

_____

_____

Suffering (fear of facing the kind of persecution Christ endured)

_____

Reluctance (withholding Christ from people different from us)

_____

_____

Comparison (comparing our path to someone else's)

_____

_____

Resistance (holding back when God calls us to lead)

_____

_____

Lukewarmness (losing our passion for Christ)

_____

_____

Indifference (an unconcerned attitude toward reaching the lost)

_____

_____

Selfishness (an unwillingness to support missionaries)

_____

_____

Carnality (allowing our fleshly nature to control us)

_____

_____

Confusion (uncertainty about God's will for our lives)

_____

What hurdle, more than all the others, do you consistently have difficulty clearing?

Why does this particular hurdle trip you up?

What specific truth from our study of Scripture have you turned to for help in overcoming this obstacle?

When an intimidating row of hurdles looms ahead, remember you don't have to clear them in your own strength. You may not be able to run the race in record-setting time or with the grace and speed of an Olympic champion. But you do have the power of the Holy Spirit. And you do have the support of fellow runners to pick you up when you fall. So stay in the race. Keep on running. You are a hurdler!

> Therefore, since we have so great a cloud of witnesses surrounding us, let us also lay aside every encumbrance, and the sin which so easily entangles us, and let us run with endurance the race that is set before us, fixing our eyes on Jesus, the author and perfecter of faith, who for the joy set before Him endured the cross, despising the shame, and has sat down at the right hand of the throne of God. (Heb. 12:1–2)

BOOKS FOR
PROBING FURTHER

The hurdlers gingerly step into the starting blocks. It's just a practice session, but they take it as seriously as the big meet. The coach blows the whistle—blast-off! A few seconds later, the runners are panting at the finish line, cooling down and reviewing their technique.

What do they do now? Unlace their shoes and head for the locker room? No, they go back to the beginning to run the race over, facing those same obstacles again and again.

Spiritually speaking, clearing a few hurdles doesn't mean the race is over. We face obstacles like suffering or reluctance or comparison again and again. Sometimes we glide over the top; other times, we stumble and crash in the dirt. But the more we stick to it, the more our maturity and strength as runners grow.

We've put together some resources to assist you on the track. These books address in more detail some of the hurdles we talked about in this study. Pick one that best applies to the obstacle you're facing right now, and see the different ways you can improve your hurdling technique.

Borthwick, Paul. *How to Be a World-Class Christian*. Wheaton, Ill.: Scripture Press Publications, Victor Books, 1991. You don't have to become a full-time missionary to reach the world for Christ. This vision-expanding book reveals ways you can help fulfill the Great Commission without leaving your backyard.

Carlisle, Thomas John. *You! Jonah!* Grand Rapids, Mich.: William B. Eerdmans Publishing Co., 1968. Carlisle's thoughtful poems provide some excellent insights into the life of Jonah—and into the Jonah within each of us.

Flynn, Leslie and Bernice. *God's Will: You Can Know It*. Wheaton, Ill.: Scripture Press Publications, Victor Books, 1979. Expanding on the insights we outlined in this study guide, the Flynns teach a method of knowing God's will that is both sensible and reliable.

Stowell, Joseph M. *Eternity: Reclaiming a Passion for What Endures*. Chicago, Ill.: Moody Press, 1995. Stowell believes we should live "life in the long view"—not thinking of eternity as a destination but as a guiding influence along the way. His book helps us learn heavenly values so we can focus our lives on the things that last.

————. *Fan the Flame*. Chicago, Ill.: Moody Press, 1986. When our love for Christ cools to a gray mound of embers, we need not despair. Stowell helps us fan the embers into a crackling fire by leading us back to Christ, the source of our passion. He also deals with fire-smothering rules in our lives, encouraging us to love God wholeheartedly and get our eyes off ourselves and onto others.

White, John. *Magnificent Obsession: The Joy of Christian Commitment*. Revised edition. Downers Grove, Ill.: InterVarsity Press, 1990. A revision of White's earlier *The Cost of Commitment* (InterVarsity, 1976), this new book reflects the author's growth, maturity, and increased passion for Christ. He's been down the track, faced the hurdle of suffering many times, and can help you find joy in the midst of suffering for the sake of Christ.

Yancey, Philip. *Disappointment with God*. Grand Rapids, Mich.: Zondervan Publishing House, 1988. Fear that God will disappoint us is one of the reasons we're reluctant to follow His call. Have you ever wondered: *Is God fair? Does He really care about me? Why does He allow me to suffer if He loves me?* Yancey spades into the Scripture and masterfully gleans truths that reveal the God of love and the love He seeks from us during the hard times.

Some of these books may be out of print and available only through a library. For those currently available, please contact your local Christian bookstore. Books by Charles R. Swindoll may be obtained through Insight for Living. IFL also offers some books by other authors—please note the ordering information that follows and contact the office that serves you.

ORDERING INFORMATION

CLEARING THE HIGH HURDLES
Cassette Tapes and Study Guide

This Bible study guide was designed to be used independently or in conjunction with the broadcast of Chuck Swindoll's taped messages which are listed below. If you would like to order cassette tapes or further copies of this study guide, please see the information given below and the order forms provided at the end of this guide.

		U.S.	Canada
CHH	Study guide	$ 4.95 ea.	$ 6.50 ea.
CHHCS	Cassette series, includes all individual tapes, album cover, and one complimentary study guide	34.75	40.75
CHH 1–5	Individual cassettes, includes messages A and B	6.00 ea.	7.48 ea.

The prices are subject to change without notice.

CHH 1-A: *Clearing the Hurdle of Unpreparedness*—
Matthew 25:1–13
    B: *Clearing the Hurdle of Suffering*—Selected Scriptures

CHH 2-A: *Clearing the Hurdle of Reluctance*—The Book of Jonah
    B: *Clearing the Hurdle of Comparison*—John 21:15–22

CHH 3-A: *Clearing the Hurdle of Resistance*—Exodus 3:1–4:18
    B: *Clearing the Hurdle of Lukewarmness*—
Revelation 3:14–20

CHH 4-A: *Clearing the Hurdle of Indifference*—Selections from Philippians
    B: *Clearing the Hurdle of Selfishness*—Selections from Philippians

CHH 5-A: *Clearing the Hurdle of Carnality*—Selections from
1 Corinthians
    B: *Clearing the Hurdle of Confusion*—Selected Scriptures

How to Order by Phone or FAX

(Credit card orders only)

United States: 1-800-772-8888 from 7:00 A.M. to 4:30 P.M., Pacific time, Monday through Friday
FAX (714) 575-5496 anytime, day or night

Canada: 1-800-663-7639, Vancouver residents call (604) 532-7172 from 8:00 A.M. to 5:00 P.M., Pacific time, Monday through Friday
FAX (604) 532-7173 anytime, day or night

Australia and the South Pacific: (03) 9-872-4606 or FAX (03) 9-874-8890 from 8:00 A.M. to 5:00 P.M., Monday through Friday

---

Other International Locations: call the Ordering Services Department in the United States at (714) 575-5000 during the hours listed above.

How to Order by Mail

United States
• Mail to: Processing Services Department
Insight for Living
Post Office Box 69000
Anaheim, CA 92817-0900
• Sales tax: California residents add 7.25%.
• Shipping and handling charges must be added to each order. See chart on order form for amount.
• Payment: personal checks, money orders, credit cards (Visa, Master-Card, Discover Card, and American Express). No invoices or COD orders available.
• $10 fee for *any* returned check.

Canada
• Mail to: Insight for Living Ministries
Post Office Box 2510
Vancouver, BC V6B 3W7
• Sales tax: please add 7% GST. British Columbia residents also add 7% sales tax (on tapes or cassette series).
• Shipping and handling charges must be added to each order. See chart on order form for amount.
• Payment: personal cheques, money orders, credit cards (Visa, Master-Card). No invoices or COD orders available.
• Delivery: approximately four weeks.

Australia and the South Pacific
- Mail to: Insight for Living, Inc.
  GPO Box 2823 EE
  Melbourne, Victoria 3001, Australia
- Shipping: add 25% to the total order.
- Delivery: approximately four to six weeks.
- Payment: personal checks payable in Australian funds, international money orders, or credit cards (Visa, MasterCard, and BankCard).

Other International Locations
- Mail to: Processing Services Department
  Insight for Living
  Post Office Box 69000
  Anaheim, CA 92817-0900
- Shipping and delivery time: please see chart that follows.
- Payment: personal checks payable in U.S. funds, international money orders, or credit cards (Visa, MasterCard, and American Express).

Type of Shipping	Postage Cost	Delivery
Surface	10% of total order*	6 to 10 weeks
Airmail	25% of total order*	under 6 weeks

Use U.S. price as a base.

Our Guarantee

Your complete satisfaction is our top priority here at Insight for Living. If you're not completely satisfied with anything you order, please return it for full credit, a refund, or a replacement, as *you* prefer.

Insight for Living Catalog

The Insight for Living catalog features study guides, tapes, and books by a variety of Christian authors. To obtain a free copy, call us at the numbers listed above.

Order Form
United States, Australia, and Other International Locations
(Canadian residents please use order form on reverse side.)

CHHCS represents the entire *Clearing the High Hurdles* series in a special album cover, while CHH 1–5 are the individual tapes included in the series. CHH represents this study guide, should you desire to order additional copies.

CHH	Study guide	$ 4.95 ea.
CHHCS	Cassette series, includes all individual tapes, album cover, and one complimentary study guide	34.75
CHH 1–5	Individual cassettes, includes messages A and B	6.00 ea.

Product Code	Product Description	Quantity	Unit Price	Total
			$	$

			Order Total

Amount of Order	First Class	UPS
$ 7.50 and under	1.00	4.00
$ 7.51 to 12.50	1.50	4.25
$12.51 to 25.00	3.50	4.50
$25.01 to 35.00	4.50	4.75
$35.01 to 60.00	5.50	5.25
$60.00 and over	6.50	5.75

UPS ❏ First Class ❏ *Shipping and handling must be added. See chart for charges.*	
Subtotal	
California Residents—Sales Tax *Add 7.25% of subtotal.*	
Non-United States Residents *Australia add 25%. All other locations: U.S. price plus 10% surface postage or 25% airmail.*	
Gift to Insight for Living *Tax-deductible in the United States.*	
Total Amount Due *Please do not send cash.*	$

Fed Ex and Fourth Class are also available. Please call for details.

If you are placing an order after January 1, 1997, please call for current prices.

Prices are subject to change without notice.

Payment by: ❏ Check or money order payable to Insight for Living ❏ Credit card

(Circle one):   Visa   MasterCard   Discover Card   American Express   BankCard (In Australia)

Number _____

Expiration Date _____   Signature _____
We cannot process your credit card purchase without your signature.

Name _____

Address _____

City _____   State _____

Zip Code _____   Country _____

Telephone (___) _____   Radio Station ____ ____ ____ ____
If questions arise concerning your order, we may need to contact you.

Mail this order form to the Processing Services Department at one of these addresses:

Insight for Living
Post Office Box 69000, Anaheim, CA 92817-0900

Insight for Living, Inc.
GPO Box 2823 EE, Melbourne, VIC 3001, Australia

ECFA MEMBER

Order Form
Canadian Residents

(Residents of the United States, Australia, and other international locations, please use order form on reverse side.)

CHHCS represents the entire *Clearing the High Hurdles* series in a special album cover, while CHH 1–5 are the individual tapes included in the series. CHH represents this study guide, should you desire to order additional copies.

CHH	Study guide	$ 6.50 ea.
CHHCS	Cassette series, includes all individual tapes, album cover, and one complimentary study guide	40.75
CHH 1–5	Individual cassettes, includes messages A and B	7.48 ea.

Product Code	Product Description	Quantity	Unit Price	Total
			$	$

Amount of Order	Canada Post
Orders to $10.00	2.00
$10.01 to 30.00	3.50
$30.01 to 50.00	5.00
$50.01 to 99.99	7.00
$100 and over	Free

Loomis is also available. Please call for details.

Subtotal	
Add 7% GST	
British Columbia Residents Add 7% sales tax on individual tapes or cassette series.	
Shipping Shipping and handling must be added. See chart for charges.	
Gift to Insight for Living Ministries Tax-deductible in Canada.	
Total Amount Due Please do not send cash.	$

Prices are subject to change without notice.

Payment by: ❑ Cheque or money order payable to Insight for Living Ministries
❑ Credit card

(Circle one): Visa   MasterCard   Number _____

Expiration Date _____   Signature _____
We cannot process your credit card purchase without your signature.

Name _____

Address _____

City _____   Province _____

Postal Code _____   Country _____

Telephone (____) _____   Radio Station ____ ____ ____ ____
If questions arise concerning your order, we may need to contact you.

Mail this order form to the Processing Services Department at the following address:

Insight for Living Ministries
Post Office Box 2510
Vancouver, BC, Canada V6B 3W7

Order Form
United States, Australia, and Other International Locations
(Canadian residents please use order form on reverse side.)

CHHCS represents the entire *Clearing the High Hurdles* series in a special album cover, while CHH 1–5 are the individual tapes included in the series. CHH represents this study guide, should you desire to order additional copies.

CHH	Study guide	$ 4.95 ea.
CHHCS	Cassette series, includes all individual tapes, album cover, and one complimentary study guide	34.75
CHH 1–5	Individual cassettes, includes messages A and B	6.00 ea.

Product Code	Product Description	Quantity	Unit Price	Total
			$	$

			Order Total	

Amount of Order	First Class	UPS		
$ 7.50 and under	1.00	4.00	**UPS ❑ First Class ❑** *Shipping and handling must be added. See chart for charges.*	
$ 7.51 to 12.50	1.50	4.25	**Subtotal**	
$12.51 to 25.00	3.50	4.50	**California Residents—Sales Tax** *Add 7.25% of subtotal.*	
$25.01 to 35.00	4.50	4.75	**Non-United States Residents** *Australia add 25%. All other locations: U.S. price plus 10% surface postage or 25% airmail.*	
$35.01 to 60.00	5.50	5.25		
$60.00 and over	6.50	5.75		

Fed Ex and Fourth Class are also available. Please call for details.

Gift to Insight for Living *Tax-deductible in the United States.*	
Total Amount Due *Please do not send cash.*	$

Prices are subject to change without notice.

Payment by: ❑ Check or money order payable to Insight for Living ❑ Credit card

(Circle one):   Visa   MasterCard   Discover Card   American Express   BankCard
(In Australia)

Number _____

Expiration Date _____   Signature _____
We cannot process your credit card purchase without your signature.

Name _____

Address _____

City _____   State _____

Zip Code _____   Country _____

Telephone (___) _____   Radio Station ____ ____ ____ ____
If questions arise concerning your order, we may need to contact you.

Mail this order form to the Processing Services Department at one of these addresses:

Insight for Living
Post Office Box 69000, Anaheim, CA 92817-0900

Insight for Living, Inc.
GPO Box 2823 EE, Melbourne, VIC 3001, Australia

ECFA MEMBER

Order Form
Canadian Residents

(Residents of the United States, Australia, and other international locations,
please use order form on reverse side.)

CHHCS represents the entire *Clearing the High Hurdles* series in a special album cover, while
CHH 1–5 are the individual tapes included in the series. CHH represents this study guide,
should you desire to order additional copies.

CHH	Study guide	$ 6.50 ea.
CHHCS	Cassette series,	40.75
	includes all individual tapes, album cover,	
	and one complimentary study guide	
CHH 1–5	Individual cassettes,	7.48 ea.
	includes messages A and B	

Product Code	Product Description	Quantity	Unit Price	Total
			$	$

Amount of Order	Canada Post		
Orders to $10.00	2.00	**Subtotal**	
$10.01 to 30.00	3.50	**Add 7% GST**	
$30.01 to 50.00	5.00	**British Columbia Residents** *Add 7% sales tax on individual tapes or cassette series.*	
$50.01 to 99.99	7.00	**Shipping** *Shipping and handling must be added. See chart for charges.*	
$100 and over	Free	**Gift to Insight for Living Ministries** *Tax-deductible in Canada.*	
		Total Amount Due *Please do not send cash.*	$

Loomis is also available. Please
call for details.

Prices are subject to change without notice.

Payment by: ❏ Cheque or money order payable to Insight for Living Ministries
❏ Credit card

(Circle one): Visa   MasterCard   Number _____

Expiration Date _____   Signature _____
We cannot process your credit card purchase without your signature.

Name _____

Address _____

City _____   Province _____

Postal Code _____   Country _____

Telephone (___) _____   Radio Station ____ ____ ____ ____
If questions arise concerning your order, we may need to contact you.

Mail this order form to the Processing Services Department at the following address:

Insight for Living Ministries
Post Office Box 2510
Vancouver, BC, Canada V6B 3W7